Agrarian Question
A Short Reader

Edited by

R.V. Ramana Murthy

AAKAR

Agrarian Question: A Short Reader
R.V. Ramana Murthy

First Published 2020

ISBN 978-93-5002-631-1

Published by
AAKAR BOOKS
28 E Pocket IV, Mayur Vihar Phase I
Delhi 110 091 India
aakarbooks@gmail.com

Laser Typeset at
Sakshi Computers, Delhi

Printed at
Sapra Brothers, Noida

To Prof. D. Narasimha Reddy

who taught Political Economy to our generation

Contents

Preface 7

Acknowledgements 9

1. Introduction 11
2. The Secret of Primitive Accumulation 27
   Karl Marx
3. Genesis of the Capitalist Farmer 33
   Karl Marx
4. Peasant Question in France and Germany 37
   Friedrich Engels
5. The Agrarian Question 51
   Karl Kautsky
6. Is Class Struggle the Prime Mover in Transition from Feudalism to Capitalism? 60
   Stephan R. Epstein
7. Is Indian Agriculture Feudal, Semi-Feudal or Capitalist? 70
   Praful Bidwai
8. Three Models of Transition from Feudalism to Capitalism: England, France and Prussia 80
   Terence J. Byres

9. Agrarian Question: 'Then' and 'Now' 92
Henry Bernstein

10. The Agrarian Question Under Globalization 109
Haroon Akram-Lodhi and Cristobel Kay

11. Capital and Non-Capital in Capitalism in India 123
Kalyan Sanyal

12. Transition in Indian Agriculture: What Does the Data Tell Us? 131
Amit Basole and Deepankar Basu

13. The Agrarian Question Under Neoliberalism and Land Reforms in India 144
Jens Lerche

14. Agrarian Conditions in Telangana and AP: Summary of Observations 168
R.V. Ramana Murthy

15. Dalits and the Land Question: A View from the Ground 177
S.R. Vidyasagar

16. The Nationalization of the Land 190
Karl Marx

About the Contributors 195

Preface

There is a renewed interest in agrarian studies in the last one decade and more in India, probably, owing to the ensuing agrarian crisis in the country and elsewhere. This has drawn many young people to take an interest to understand and are even prepared to go to villages and work on farmers' issues. The second important constituency of the agrarian question is the left movement. Most of the left parties have not re-examined their position regarding peasants as the transformatory class in the socialist movement, issues of their mobilization, the role of the agrarian sector in the overall capitalist economy, as well as on the nature of relations of production. Agriculture in the past three decades has undergone a substantial change in its character. Even while uneven development of agriculture is still a major feature of Indian agriculture, the direction of the movement of change in several regions is clearer now than in the past. There is a desperate need to reorganize the structure of agrarian production to deal with many of its critical problems like declining viability, stagnating capital formation, environmental degradation and marginalized existence under global supply chains. The democratic transformation is further constrained as the public policy underwent a full circle, from free markets to intervention and back to free markets as the broad framework of development. Both, the political and the developmental question of agrarian change, needs a systemic perspective on political economy of capitalist development. The scholarly literature is usually spread among a number of books and journals, which is sometimes voluminous. The modest objective of this reader is to bring them to one place and introduce them in summary form, so that it helps one to get a quick view of the central issue in the agrarian change in capitalist development. This reader can be readily used by teachers in agrarian studies' courses at undergraduate and graduate studies in economics, sociology and anthropology. The reader can be useful for activists and researchers who want to gain a primary understanding of the agrarian question. Since, all these presented here are summaries of originally longer versions, as an editor I have to concede that they may seem incomplete. Readers who wish to delve deep into the issues, are advised to refer to the original versions for a fuller understanding.

October 25, 2019 R.V.R.M.

Acknowledgements

I express my sincere gratitude to the authors who have appreciated this idea of the reader on the agrarian question and gracefully agreed to give the permissions to publish the summary versions of their articles. Most of these summaries have appeared in the special issue on 'Agrarian Relations: A Long Debate' in *Broadsheet on Contemporary Politics*, journal published by Anveshi, Research Centre for Womens' Studies, Hyderabad in 2018 that has received considerable appreciation. I am grateful to them for giving the permission to print the revised versions of these in this reader. My special thanks to Suneetha who has taken considerable pains in editing the initial drafts. I am indebted to Srivats whose engagement has shaped this reader. I express my gratitude to my friends in his journey S.R. Vidyasagar and Bhargava Gadiyaram, who supported this project with their scholarship with conviction. I am also grateful to my friends V. Janardhan and Arun Patnaik whose intellectual companionship is invaluable to me. I am thankful to Dr. R. Srivatsan who has summarised Kalyan Sanyal's work. Finally, I thank the copy editor Ms. Jehanara Wasi, who have taken pains to clean up the drafts and Aakar Books for readily agreeing to publish this reader.

R.V. Ramana Murthy

1

Introduction

The agrarian question is a term coined by the German Marxist Karl Kautsky that refers to the process of transition of relations of production in agriculture from pre-capitalist to capitalist mode of production; its role and significance for overall capitalist development of the economy and the fate of small peasantry in this process. This is an extremely useful way to understand the prospects of the agricultural sector, problems of the different classes of farmers, various crises that the sector undergoes, and the institutional solutions. The conventional understanding of economic development suggests that the agricultural sector plays a pivotal role in terms of supplying the agricultural surplus to the modern sector, sustain its wages by keeping the food prices low, and earn foreign exchange through exports, etc. It is also the biggest source of employment. The surplus labour of the sector is also the source of keeping the wages low for the modern sector and accumulate. Thus, a much larger role of the agricultural sector is contemplated for the development of the economy as a whole. State intervention to protect the agricultural markets had been the corollary for the development model. This perspective seemed to have altered radically since the last few decades after globalization.

Agricultural surplus is no longer considered necessary for the modern sector in the globalized regime. The ownership structure, characterized by huge inequality, makes livelihoods difficult for the vast majority of the peasants, while adverse terms of trade, dwindling protection from international trade, declining access to institutional credit, technology, infrastructure, and ecological barriers begin to pose an existential crisis for a greater portion of the peasantry. The prospects of the farmers now depend on the configuration of the relations of production, brute forces of supply and demand. Surplus populations are not absorbed into the expanding modern sector, as it happened in the developed capitalist countries at some historical point, in this sense the agrarian question is said to have been resolved. In the absence of such a resolution, what is the course of agrarian change in developing countries? The political economy of the agrarian question alone provides a comprehensive framework to understand this challenge.

In the recent times, the agrarian crisis in India in particular has attracted considerable attention both from academics and social activists. Such an agrarian crisis has been taking place in the face of substantial growth of production, rise in average productivity, and capital formation. The character of the production process, across the country, also has changed towards more and more commercial forms. Production for more exchange than for self-consumption, suggesting a change from a largely subsistence character, centred on food crops, to a range of non-food crops, whose markets are integrated with national and global markets. Agriculture also is supported by a good deal of institutional finance, mechanization of operations as well as irrigation, and modern inputs that are often supplied by multinational corporations. This transformation kept the production and productivity going. However, agriculture as a sector remained centred around petty commodity producers, given the lack of a requisite labour absorption into the non-agricultural sector. This transformation also brought in considerable class differentiation, even if not in terms of land ownership, but in ownership of tools, investment and value added. Medium and large peasants have diversified towards more investment intensive activities, while hordes of small peasantry are caught in low-investment crops and activities. Even as agricultural production as a whole has been experiencing an occasional crisis of viability, it is the the small peasantry which is facing this crisis more frequently. The literature on the agrarian question investigates all these aspects and is an extremely useful guide to analyse these issues. This reader aims to help the young scholars who are attempting to grapple with the issues of contemporary agriculture.

Scholarship on agrarian change also needs to understand the political economy of the contemporary rural society. The capitalist development in the rural economy would push the accumulating classes to channel their surpluses into newer activities, grab opportunities outside traditional arenas and make new capital investments. Construction, roads, agri-business, cold-chains, retail, processing, finance, real estate would eventually absorb the agrarian surplus, to the extent where dominant sections of farmers are exiting agricultural production. The growing petty commoditization of agriculture in several parts of India is indicative of this process. While this certainly leads to the structural transformation in terms of income generation and distribution, the structural transformation of agrarian labour seems to be fluid. This process is likely to shape the politics and economics of the development question in the poor countries. What are future possibilities and limits of this transformative process? Once again, important clues to this question can be found in the literature on the agrarian question.

Understanding the nature of agrarian transition is an imperative for any socialist movement which plans to build an egalitarian society. The task of mobilizing the revolutionary classes requires an understanding of the transformatory potential of those classes. Social democratic parties have always had to grapple with the peasant question whose ambiguous existence in terms of class–understood both as a working and a capitalist class needs scientific analysis–in deductive and inductive terms. Reading of classical scholarly works of the past and the present with a fresh perspective is necessary, to imagine the necessary class alliances for the emancipatory project of socialism.

With the kind of concerns elicited above, this reader will attempt to answer ten important questions on agrarian change. It begins with, first, looking at the English experience, where Marx narrates the emergence of the capitalist farmer and the decline of small peasantry. Marx's influential essay proposes a notion of historical transition of agrarian structure. It asks, in such a transition, what would be the 'prime mover'? The essay served as a template for many later scholars who studied English and other agrarian transitions focusing on the model of transition and the question of the prime mover.

But then, can the English case be generalized to explain every other transition? If there is no one generalizable experience, the next question arises as to what the different historical experiences in agrarian transition are. The subsequent question is that, even if the experience of capitalist transition proves to be different in terms of sequencing and spacing, what are the common features in diverse patterns? Following this, one also needs to ask, as we know that capitalist development proceeded from an age of imperialism/colonialism to post-colonial capitalism, forming a hierarchy between centre and periphery. What are the differences in agrarian change in these two temporally different geopolitical spheres? In the post-colonial phase of capitalist development and later, under globalization, has the salience of the agrarian question remained the same or has it changed substantially? If it has changed, it brings us to the last question, how else should the agrarian question be defined now?

After posing these conceptual questions, we turn to the next set of questions concerning the Indian transition since the formation of the Indian nation-state. What are the take-aways from the 'Great Indian Mode of Production Debate' that took place in the 1970s? Even if the first three decades did not bring adequate clarity on the question, did clarity emerge from reflecting on the changes that took place in the last three decades, after the neoliberal reforms? The reader will throw some light on the emerging structure of capitalist development in the post-colonial condition, as well as concrete changes in the modes of production, structures of accumulation and social relations of production. Another issue that it will address is how the Indian Left has analysed these changes for their programmatic agenda. Finally, is there a final resolution for the agrarian question, in any sense?

The reader presents fourteen short summaries of important works, which have appeared in the form of long essays, books, and articles in professional journals. The idea is to introduce young scholars and students, especially from India, quickly to a debate which is spread across a large body of literature that occurred over decades. As such, this reader can only show the broad direction of the debate and may suffer from some transmission loss in the original ideas conveyed by the authors. Therefore, the default advice to one who gets seriously interested in the debate is to always go back and read the original works, whose references are available here. The set of readings chosen here would, it is hoped, answer the questions raised above in a substantial way. I shall only introduce them here briefly.

Marx's Initiation

To begin, Marx the originator of the idea, is relevant for making initiation as well as the final point. The debate on the agrarian transition to capitalism arises from the two essays that Marx wrote 'Genesis of Capitalist Farmer' [*Capital*, Vol. I, pp. 743-4]. 'The Secret of Primitive Accumulation' [*Capital*, Vol. III, pp. 713-6], which are presented as Chapters 2 and 3. Marx traced the particular circumstances that gave rise to the capitalist farmer in 16th century England. He narrates the historical events of the rise of agricultural prices in the 14th century, enclosures by the landlords, displacement of small peasants, the Black Death and its consequences of collapse of tenancy, and eventual emergence of the middle level tenant farmer as the capitalist farmer leasing in land, hiring wage labour and earning a profit from trade. Marx also discusses the accompanying factors for the emergence of such a system. Somehow, in popular literature this is sometimes taken as the classical route of the capitalist transformation–template to follow, even though Marx never said this. His observations on the English experience of primitive accumulation and capitalist transition in the sense of elimination of the small peasantry, transforming them into either capitalist farmers or proletariat did not exactly get repeated elsewhere. Marx's essays are necessary to understand the germination of the idea of the agrarian question and its resolution, to begin with, as Marxists pose.

Agrarian Change and Conditions of Small Peasants

After Marx's death, French and German social democratic parties faced the dilemma, which arises from the fact that the resolution of the agrarian question is not just an event, but a process in completion. This poses the challenge of organizing the small peasantry, a class who are substantial in number, yet generally indifferent towards democratic politics at the national level. Despite, facing periodic crises of viability, small peasants tenaciously survived the ruthlessly destructive competitive conditions. Engel's *Peasant Question in France and Germany*, written slightly earlier than Kautsky's work in 1894 addresses precisely this predicament faced by the Social Democratic Parties. Engels clearly conveyed the indefensibility of the small peasant position under capitalist competition, warned the SDP not to give false promises, at the same time, and suggested not leaving them to the bourgeois leadership. There are several smaller institutional measures that can be undertaken by the bourgeois state that give a breather to the small peasant. He emphasizes the need to organize the peasants into cooperatives as the only measure that can offer a limited solution to peasants, who otherwise would be wiped out. Chapter 4 presents the short version of this seminal work, that every student of the agrarian question should read, titled *Peasant Question in France and Germany* (1894).

Kautsky's book *Die Agrefrage* (*The Agrarian Question,* 1886) was perhaps the first comprehensive work on transformation of agriculture under the influence of industrial capitalism. He also dealt, conceptually and empirically, with the question that there could be no death of small peasants, but a dogged persistence, despite industrialization, as happened in Germany. Indeed industrial development would hasten the transformation of agriculture, even if it is delayed. Lenin regarded Kautksy's work as the most original and important. His own work on *Development of Capitalism in Russian Agriculture* in 1904 was, on his own admission a restatement of Kautsky's thesis in the Russian context. Somehow, Lenin's work overshadowed Kautsky's book, though his work was built entirely on the framework of the latter. Kautksy's writings become extremely useful to understand the Indian context, especially for the kind of agrarian transition that occurred under the efforts in the Indian state in the first four decades since independence. Kautsky's conclusion that agrarian transition does not mean total elimination of small and marginal peasantry from agriculture; that those who tend to survive through self-exploitation and starvation as a means to avoid joining the reserve army of labour, is instructive to everyone who examines this question. Their formal subsumption into the capitalist accumulation process that enables the extraction of surplus value from their family labour, which is highlighted by scholars in the later period, can be found implicit in Kautsky's work. Five crucial chapters of Kautsky's book are summarized and presented in Chapter 5.

How Did Capitalism Emerge From Feudalism?

The debate over the revolutionary strategy for socialism recurred in the post-world war period of decolonization, which again centred on the issue of transition of pre-capitalist societies into capitalist ones. The influence of European Marxists remained strong over the Third World Marxists, which shaped the debate. A search for determinants of transition in Europe was undertaken for the possible lessons for others, broadly in terms of structure versus agency. Whether the changes are a result of gradual changes in structure or action of resisting classes alluded to give clues for the present. For instance, the position taken by two English historians, Maurice Dobb and Rodney Hilton, held considerable influence on the transition discourse. The grand debate over what constitutes the prime mover in transition between Dobb-Hilton and Paul Sweezy, is an important engagement in the agrarian question discourse.

It draws our attention to the complex interplay of internal and external factors, which needs be understood in terms of what Marx aptly called 'uneven and combined development'. The paper by Stefan Epstein critically evaluates Dobb-Hilton's English-centric position and reconciles with the other factors such as long distance trade, technology, and role of state, which brought the change along with the class struggle. Chapter 6 presents the short version of his article, which becomes important to see its ramifications even for the contemporary times. Thus this broadens our idea of the prime mover in the discourse of transition.

The Indian Mode of Production Debate

The great Indian mode of production debate that took place in the mid-1970s probably was the last intellectual attempt in India to seriously debate the nature of the mode of production in the Indian economy in general and in Indian agriculture in particular. This extended debate, which involved over two dozen political economists and largely remained academic and confined to a few who cared to read the frustratingly polemical essays, remained inconclusive given the vast diversity of Indian agricultural forms. The debate centred on how to characterize the nature of accumulation: whether it is essentially 'capitalist' or 'semi-feudal/ semi-colonial' or 'feudal'. The enormous theoretical and empirical work, which appeared in the issues of *Economic and Political Weekly* and other journals in India was largely based on the classical theory of transition. On a positive note, one can say that it brought out the complexity of the question–whether one should identify a set of practices of farmers and attributes of the system to characterize the generic nature of the system. It also reflected the influence of the Dobb-Sweezy debate, neo-Marxian critiques on one hand and certain particular agrarian relations as necessarily pre-capitalist or semi-feudal. We have a short summary of a review written by Praful Bidwai, and published as an appendix in his posthumous book titled *The Phoenix Moment* (2015) in Chapter 7. As the author writes, the subsequent scholarly work on different states in India has brought more clarity on the diversity as well as convergence in the past three decades. Reading this debate now would refresh our understanding of the limits and contours in which the discourse was conducted, and which therefore remained inconclusive.

Is There a Classical Transition Theory?

The non-linearity of capitalist transition, in which it is so important to see the multiple possible routes, is highlighted by the work of T.J. Byres, a well-known Marxist scholar and the founding editor for *The Journal of Peasant Studies*. Byres narrates the three distinct routes of transition to capitalism in England, France and Germany, with an essential purpose to remind us that none of them are necessarily the models of transition to repeat. Byres terms the English experience which made the middle level tenant farmer emerge as a capitalist farmer with several factors leading to this outcome, 'capitalism from below'. The French agrarian structure gave rise to a preponderance of small peasantry, who were squeezed by a large class of absentee *rentiers* through middlemen, and who were freed only after the French Revolution, transformed into capitalist farmers–all this without necessarily forming large farms. Some perished and many survived. Byres describes this as a case of 'capitalism delayed'. The third case of Prussian transition shows the case of late feudalization of peasantry by large land-owning *Junkers*, whose resistance to the Napoleonic wars, is met with a strategy of commercialization and eventual mechanization in the late 19th century, industrialization achieved through territorial expansion and state intervention, as a case of 'capitalism from above'. Byres' paper is an important one to understand the contingent nature of the capitalist transition, without essentializing any one model. In his subsequent work, Byres analysed the Russian, American, Japanese, South Korean and Indian paths highlighting the non-linearity. In the length and breadth of his works, Byres brought out the nuances and rich insights on the nature of the role that landed classes have played historically, both progressive and reactionary. More importantly, the role of the state played in mediating the class interests to accelerate the capitalist development is systematically studied by Byres. Byres in this article titled 'The Peasantry and the Development of Capitalism in Comparative Perspective' (2006) presented in Chapter 8, persuasively argues not to look for any of the models to replicate anywhere.

The Peasant Question in the 20th Century and the Capitalist Development

Bernstein's work *Agrarian Question: Now and Then* (1996) is probably the single most important writing which brings clarity on what actually the agrarian question constitutes. Drawing on Byres' exhaustive work on agrarian transition, both on the transition in the metropolis and periphery, Bernstein raises the fundamental question on the salience of posing it in a classical way. He analytically separates the agrarian question into three questions within. First is what Engels, Kautsky and Lenin dealt with in the 19th century regarding mobilization of the peasants, mostly petty commodity producers, along with workers for social democracy. He calls it the Agrarian Question of politics (AQ1). The second is that of transformation of agriculture, much needed for the progress and accumulation of industry, which also arose in the context of the Soviet Union in 1927, famously argued by its protagonist, Preobrazensky, seeking to raise cheap agricultural surplus for the urban population and to facilitate faster industrial accumulation, that Bernstein calls the AQ2. The nature of response of landlords in different countries determined how well this question was resolved, Berstein explains, taking the case of Germany, US and Japan. This issue also affected Indian development deeply, before and after the introduction of the Green Revolution. Bernstein argues that resolving the AQ1 was seen as necessary for the AQ2, as long as resolving the AQ2 was necessary. However, after globalization, when capital in the periphery got access to transnational capital, and the global food market became active, the AQ2 is not seen as necessary and so is being bypassed. Now, under globalization, as agrarian markets are reintegrated with global supply chains, organized by big capital, far more peasants across the world are incorporated into capital accumulation on a world scale. This offers no succour to the peasants who are now squeezed by global markets, are caught in pauperization but are abandoned by the state. Thus the agrarian question of labour, which, Bernstein called the AQ3, a question of social justice and democracy, remains to be resolved. And it is not going to be resolved in the way it was resolved in the developed countries. Therefore, to raise the agrarian question in a classical way of resolving the AQ2, which is a dominant practice in literature and politics, has lost its relevance. In other words the traditional agrarian question is bypassed by the globalized capital accumulation regime. This is perhaps the single most important proposition of Bernstein's article in Chapter 9 which explains the globalization process and plight of peasants across regions.

Agrarian Question in the Post-Globalization Period

One of the best review articles on the agrarian question, covering a range of questions and studies, perhaps, is that by Akram-Lodhi and Christobel Kay (2010). In their exhaustive review titled 'Surveying the Agrarian Question' in the *Journal of Peasant Studies*, they endorse Bernstein's propositions and reiterate the need for reconfiguring the agrarian question in the post-globalization period. When the agricultural sector is losing its role as complementary sector and is no longer a constraint on structural transformation, the agrarian question has no resolution in the emerging capitalist regime. Internationalization of capital is argued to have 'decoupled' the national labour regimes from transnational capital. This is not to deny the existence of an agrarian crisis, but the system has neither the need nor the compulsion to resolve it. It can draw peasants into the accumulation chain at will and abandon them through market mayhem during harvest bounties. In terms of livelihood crises undoubtedly the agrarian question remains. Akram-Lodhi and Kay further suggest that one should even expand its scope by introducing gender and ecological aspects. Building on Bernstien, Akram Lodhi-Kay argue that analytically the agrarian question is indeed to be split into eight questions, by adding on food regime, gender, ecology, classes of labour, and political ecology. The summarized version of their two-part article is presented in Chapter 10. The agrarian question is reloaded in a wider context by Akram-Lodhi and Kay.

Capitalist Development in India: Post-Mode of Production Debate Views

To come to terms with the trajectory of India's particular capitalist transition, it would be far more important to look into the structure and nature. The Indian transition case highlights the role played by the post-colonial developmental state. We introduce an important and interesting work of the late Kalyan Sanyal, *Rethinking Capitalist Development: Primitive Accumulation, Governmentality and the Post-Colonial Capitalism* (2007) in Chapter 11. Tracing the diligent efforts of the developmental state in the post-independence period, through planning and intervention, Sanyal shows how it raised the resources, eased the constraints of growth and expanded capitalist architecture in India. Sanyal highlights the peculiar economic and political conditions of 20th century post-colonial capitalism, which are distinct from the conditions under which Western capitalism was incubated. Here lack of conditions for classical transition to industrial economy leads to the creation of the informal sector, which is the quintessential post-colonial condition. Sanyal reconceptualizes surplus labour in the economy, as they migrate to the urban informal sector, as the non-capital sector, which remains tethered to the capitalist sector even as it is rejected from formal incorporation. He argues that this management of the conditions of capitalist political economy is a typical post-colonial feature. The political process of establishing hegemony over such labour through *governmentality*–a Foucaultian idea of how a modern liberal state manages the various population groups through welfare programmes, without yielding any formal rights, constitutes the politics of the nation state. A provocative yet extremely scholarly argument by Sanyal, we introduce it with a wafer thin summary interpretation which should inspire serious readers to read the original.

How much has Indian agriculture actually changed in broad terms? An impressive account provided by a significant study by Amit Basole and Deepankar Basu (2011) that brought out the empirical developments in the past five decades is presented in Chapter 12. Based on the National Sample Survey data during (1961-2011), the authors set out to identify the dominant mode of surplus appropriation. While their original article has two parts, one on agriculture and the other on industry, we present the findings of Part I, relevant for our purpose. While taking it for granted that the dominant mode of accumulation in the modern sector (industry and service sector) is through exploitation of wage labour as in any standard capitalist system, they proceed to map out the situation for agriculture. They argue that in spite of the trend of acute fragmentation of holdings and rise of small/marginal holdings, all other features indicate unambiguously capitalist economy. Important trends are a rise in capital formation in agriculture, increased share of institutional credit, falling share of agricultural income for rural households for poorer households in particular, replaced with wage income from farm and non-farm sources, rise in self-cultivation, reduced share of tenancy, rise in cash rents, and so on. The authors muster impressive macro evidence to suggest that Indian agriculture made definite strides towards capitalist relations and dominant mode of surplus extraction is wage labour exploitation. Agriculture by becoming commercial does not necessarily become remunerative for lower strands of peasantry, is indeed a logical outcome of class differentiation.

What are the positions of the Indian political Left on the agrarian question, its resolution and their strategies of mobilization? India's main left parties have entrenched themselves around characterizing the nature of agrarian structure as 'semi-feudal', with shades of differences between the Communist Party of India-Marxist (CPM) and the Communist Party of India-Marxist-Leninist (CPI-ML), where the former acknowledges the significant growth of capitalist relations in agriculture, while the latter locks itself in a denial mode. These positions arrived at almost five decades ago, remain mostly unchanged even now. Echoing the party positions, academic positions sympathetic to the parties maintain a more or less similar discourse. Jens Lerche, an academic and currently the editor of *The Journal of Agrarian Change*, challenges these positions with the help of extensive review of studies and data. He argues that the understanding of the dominant Left in India is rooted in the classical model of transition, which needs to be revised since the classical agrarian question is bypassed in the era of globalization,–a la Bernstein. Further, he questions the primacy given to the issue of redistributive land reforms, Besides the question of availability of surplus land, he argues that they no longer have a role in resolving the agrarian question of capital. The agrarian question of labour, whether landed or landless, has to be raised from political mobilization of the masses against the dominant capital, forcing the state to mediate the contradictions between the big capital–global and local, and classes of labour exploited–directly and indirectly. Chapter 13 presents the summary of the article by Jens Lerche.

Supplementing the macro trends, there are several micro level studies on agrarian transition. The paper by R.V. Ramana Murthy in Chapter 14, brings evidence for the changing agrarian structure, endangered viability of small peasant farming, transition to non-farm activities and state welfare support to rural households from the countryside. The author presents observations from primary data on 1057 farm households in seven villages in (the erstwhile) state of Andhra Pradesh, collected in 2013. The paper supports the macro level observations on proliferation of the share of petty commodity production, non-viability of small farms on full cost, diversification of livelihood into non-farm activities and so on. The author shows that there is a growing class differentiation between two broad classes of farmers, namely those owning below 10 acres and those who own above, the former are characterized as petty commodity producers and the latter as capitalist farmers, using Utsa Patnaik's labour exploitation criterion. The former combine wage income with farm income, earn a subsistence income from a simple reproduction of value, while the latter indulge in profitable farming with expanded reproduction of value. The paper reiterates Kalyan Sanyal's position that the social welfare transfer in the current neoliberal age by the state appears to mitigate the subsistence crisis of petty commodity producing class, constitute (??/) the politics of transformation and management of poverty.

Resonating the views on development of capitalist relations, Vidyasagar's paper in Chapter 15 presents 'Dalits and the Land Question in India: A View from the Ground'. It gives the social dimension of Indian peasantry by presenting the situation of Dalits, the pariahs of the caste system. Dalits[1] were historically denied ownership of land in Indian society. The efforts of the Indian state to transfer some land to them were thoroughly defeated by the upper peasant castes. The majority of Dalits could not retain even the small parcels given to them, were compelled to sell them back to the upper peasantry and go back to wage labour. The paper argues that the overall faster capitalist growth in the economy since the 1990s has created opportunities for Dalits to escape from the countryside, its social oppression and unfree labour relations as the *attached labour*. The migration opportunities are seen to provide escape to free wage labour in urban locations, even as circulatory labour. Interesting empirical case studies are supplemented in the narrative. The author suggests that the failure of redistributive land reforms, in case of Dalits, shows the systematic bias in society as well as the exigencies of capitalist transformation that slay the holdings of the weakest section of society.

Finally, we present the small but a classic essay by Karl Marx on 'Nationalization of Land', a paper read at the Manchester Section of the International Working Men's Association in 1872, in Chapter 16. The paper clearly indicates that the agrarian sector does not have a bright future under industrial capitalism. Land reforms or market support or external markets are going to give a temporarily stable condition for the sector, which is bound to undergo crises of marginalization and pauperization. Organizing cooperatives may provide an intermediate solution, as emphasized by Engels and Kautsky, but may still not provide the final solution. Marx indicates that the final solution is sought only in the eventual nationalization of land and redistribution of national income to those engaged in the sector. This paper highlights clearly the Marxist view on the agrarian question, which cannot escape an intellectual consideration.

Final Remarks

This short reader, aimed at the young scholars and activists of the agrarian question, introduces one to many of the significant debates. It is important to be aware of changing conditions on the ground. The understanding of the capitalist system and the political discourse on agrarian issues are closely connected to each other and any fractured analysis would only slip into populism. The bourgeois economics treats farmers as rational agents and is incapable of theorizing the institutional process of peasants transforming into commercial farmers. The liberal bourgeois state which allows unfettered market forces to operate often promises to look into problems of the farming sector, only to renege on them after raising expectations, leaving people often confused whether to blame markets or state or the concerted interplay of the two. It will offer welfare transfers as a mitigating factor to deal with the political fallout. One should clearly understand that agriculture gets transformed for the capital accumulation in industrial and service sectors, hence becomes subordinated to hegemony of the latter. Second, the unequal exchange relation between the two is the source of crisis for the agrarian sector. Third, historical factors determine the nature and quantum of transformation. The eventual solution lies in socialization or nationalization of property in general, redistribution of value. All solutions that take place under capitalist relations are temporary and incomplete. We hope these articles help in building our collective understanding to think further.

NOTE

1. Dalits in India are the socially marginalized caste in the social hierarchy, who historically suffered untouchability, barred from owning land, access to literacy.

REFERENCES

Dobb, M.H., 1946. *Studies in the Development of Capitalism*, London.

Hilton, Rodney, 1978. *The Transition from Feudalism to Capitalism*, Verso, London.

2

The Secret of Primitive Accumulation

[Karl Marx]

Marx recollects for us how money becomes capital when it is invested, how this generates surplus value which is realized as profit, and how profit is reinvested as capital. However this kind of build up of capital presupposes the system of capitalist production (private enterprise), this system of capitalist production presupposes (depends on) the pre-existence of many labourers who then sell their labour power to the capitalists who produce commodities. So capital is dependent on profit is dependent on capitalist production is dependent on labourers, is dependent on capitalist production (again). How do we get out of this circular system of presuppositions? By supposing that something called primitive accumulation existed before it, i.e. a form of accumulation that occurred before capitalist production, providing a starting point.

We have seen how money is changed into capital; how through capital surplus-value is made, and from surplus-value more capital. But the accumulation of capital presupposes surplus-value; surplus-value presupposes capitalistic production; capitalistic production presupposes the pre-existence of considerable masses of capital and of labour-power in the hands of producers of commodities. The whole movement, therefore, seems to turn in a vicious circle, out of which we can only get by supposing a primitive accumulation (previous accumulation of Adam Smith) preceding capitalistic accumulation; an accumulation not the result of the capitalistic mode of production but its starting point.

This primitive accumulation plays in political economy about the same part as original sin in theology. Adam bit the apple, and thereupon sin fell on the human race. Its origin is supposed to be explained when it is told as an anecdote of the past. In times long gone by there were two sorts of people; one, the diligent, intelligent, and, above all, frugal elite; the other, lazy rascals, spending their substance, and more, in riotous living. The legend of theological original sin tells us certainly how man came to be condemned to eat his bread through the sweat of his brow; but the history of economic original sin reveals to us that there are people to whom this is by no means essential. Never mind! Thus it came to pass that the former sort accumulated wealth, and the latter sort had at last nothing to sell except their own skins. And from this original sin dates the poverty of the great majority that, despite all its labour, has up to now nothing to sell but itself, and the wealth of the few that increases constantly although they have long ceased to work. Such insipid childishness is every day preached to us in the defence of property. M. Thiers, for example, had the assurance to repeat it with all the solemnity of a statesman, to the French people, once so *spirituel*. But as soon as the question of property crops up, it becomes a sacred duty to proclaim the intellectual food of the infant as the one thing fit for all ages and for all stages of development. In actual history it is notorious that conquest, enslavement, robbery, murder, briefly force, play the great part. In the tender annals of Political Economy, the idyllic reigns from time immemorial. Right and "labour" were from all time the sole means of enrichment, the present year of course always excepted. As a matter of fact, the methods of primitive accumulation are anything but idyllic.

[This primitive accumulation is explained in capitalist theories of political economy by all kinds of fairy tales fit for children. Those who worked saved their money and became capitalists, while those who spent money and had fun became labourers. These fairy tales are used to defend the notion of private property–so that private property is the right of those who worked hard for it. But, Marx says, private property before capital was nothing but the result of violence and coercion–"conquest, enslavement, robbery, murder". In bourgeois political economy the fantasy from time

immemorial was that property was the right of the industrious. In truth and in history, primitive accumulation of property was anything but a fairy tale: violent, bloody loot.]

In themselves money and commodities are no more capital than are the means of production and of subsistence. They want transforming into capital. But this transformation itself can only take place under certain circumstances that centre in this, viz. that two very different kinds of commodity-possessors must come face to face and into contact; on the one hand, the owners of money, means of production, means of subsistence, who are eager to increase the sum of values they possess, by buying other people's labour-power; on the other hand, free labourers, the sellers of their own labour-power, and therefore the sellers of labour. Free labourers, in the double sense that neither they themselves form part and parcel of the means of production, as in the case of slaves, bondsmen, etc., nor do the means of production belong to them, as in the case of peasant-proprietors; they are, therefore, free from, unencumbered by, any means of production of their own. With this polarization of the market for commodities, the fundamental conditions of capitalist production are given. The capitalist system pre-supposes the complete separation of the labourers from all property in the means by which they can realize their labour. As soon as capitalist production is once on its own legs, it not only maintains this separation, but reproduces it on a continually extending scale. The process, therefore, that clears the way for the capitalist system, can be none other than the process which takes away from the labourer the possession of his means of production; a process that transforms, on the one hand, the social means of subsistence and of production into capital, on the other, the immediate producers into wage-labourers. The so-called primitive accumulation, therefore, is nothing else than the historical process of divorcing the producer from the means of production. It appears as primitive, because it forms the prehistoric stage of capital and the mode of production corresponding with it.

[Money, commodities, labour and production by themselves cannot create capital. Capital becomes possible only when owners of money and

commodities who require labour face labourers who don't have anything but their labour to sell. Primitive accumulation is actually the process by which both owners of money and commodities and labourers who don't have anything to sell, anywhere to go, any right except to sell their labour simultaneously are generated. It seems to be 'primitive' because it is historically the basis of capitalist production–it is capitalism's prehistory].

The economic structure of capitalistic society has grown out of the economic structure of feudal society. The dissolution of the latter set free the elements of the former.

[Capitalist society develops out of feudal society. When feudal society reaches its limits, it dissolves in its own contradictions and thus sets free the conditions that enable capitalism]

The immediate producer, the labourer, could only dispose of his own person after he had ceased to be attached to the soil and ceased to be the slave, serf, or bondsman of another. To become a free seller of labour-power, who carries his commodity wherever he finds a market, he must further have escaped from the regime of guilds, their rules for apprentices and journeymen, and the impediments of their labour regulations. Hence, the historical movement which changes the producers into wage-workers, appears, on the one hand, as their emancipation from serfdom and from the fetters of the guilds, and this side alone exists for our bourgeois historians. But, on the other hand, these new freed men became sellers of themselves only after they had been robbed of all their own means of production, and of all the guarantees of existence afforded by the old feudal arrangements. And the history of this, their expropriation, is written in the annals of mankind in letters of blood and fire.

[Labour in feudalism was in one way or other bonded to the feudal owners or lords. There were many non-economic links that forced labourers to work for their masters (landlords, guild owners, master craftsmen)–rules and regulations that were based on obligation and force. The labourer in capitalism needs to sell his labour for a wage. Wage labour is possible only when the bondsman of feudalism is freed from coercive bondage. This is the story of freedom told by bourgeois historians. The other side of the coin

is that the freedom of the labourers is the same as stripping them of their means of production, and cancelling all obligations and guarantees of survival which feudalism provided the poor. The story of this 'freedom' of their expropriation is a history of blood and fire.]

The industrial capitalists, these new potentates, had on their part not only to displace the guild masters of handicrafts, but also the feudal lords, the possessors of the sources of wealth. In this respect their conquest of social power appears as the fruit of a victorious struggle both against feudal lordship and its revolting prerogatives, and against the guilds and the fetters they laid on the free development of production and the free exploitation of man by man. The chevaliers d'industrie, however, only succeeded in supplanting the chevaliers of the sword by making use of events of which they themselves were wholly innocent. They have risen by means as vile as those by which the Roman freed man once on a time made himself the master of his *patronus*.

[Capitalists, the new powerful, had also to displace the old powerful– the guild masters, the feudal lords and the old wealthy. This story is told by bourgeois historians as a freedom of the individual from old forms of privilege through victorious struggle against injustice, against fetters on free enterprise and free labour. However, in actuality, this freedom was achieved by capitalists not by their own efforts, nor by direct intention, and often by means as dirty and scheming as in the ways in which lords came to power in earlier times in history.]

The starting-point of the development that gave rise to the wage-labourer as well as to the capitalist, was the servitude of the labourer. The advance consisted in a change of form of this servitude, in the transformation of feudal exploitation into capitalist exploitation. To understand its march, we need not go back very far. Although we come across the first beginnings of capitalist production as early as the 14th or 15th century, sporadically, in certain towns of the Mediterranean, the capitalistic era dates from the 16th century. Wherever it appears, the abolition of serfdom has been long effected, and the highest development of the middle ages, the existence of sovereign towns, has been long on the wane.

[Capitalism develops when wage labour as a form of slavery comes into being. Though early signs appear in 14th and 15th century Europe, the capitalist era begins from the 16th century. Wherever capitalism appears, serf labour or bonded slavery has been abolished and the existence of sovereign towns based on the economy of the guilds of the feudal era have begun to disappear.]

In the history of primitive accumulation, all revolutions are epoch-making that act as levers for the capitalist class in course of formation; but, above all, those moments when great masses of men are suddenly and forcibly torn from their means of subsistence, and hurled as free and "unattached" proletarians on the labour-market. The expropriation of the agricultural producer, of the peasant, from the soil, is the basis of the whole process. The history of this expropriation, in different countries, assumes different aspects, and runs through its various phases in different orders of succession, and at different periods. In England alone, which we take as our example, has the classic form.[1]

[The capitalist epoch comes into being through several revolutions that act as levers for the capitalist class as it comes into force. However, the most important of these moments is when great masses of men are thrown suddenly and forcibly into the marketplace as proletarians who sell their labour. Thus agricultural producers (peasants) who are torn from the soil (in other words, 'expropriated') and made proletarians are the first, fundamental step in the whole process. This process of expropriation differs in different countries, it has different aspects and phases, different orders of succession and occurs at different times. England alone is the classic form].

Karl Marx, *Capital*, Vol. 1, Part VIII: "The So-called Primitive Accumulation", Chapter XXVI, Moscow: Progress Publishers, 1965, pp. 713-716.

3

Genesis of the Capitalist Farmer

[Karl Marx]

Now that we have considered the forcible creation of a class of outlawed proletarians, the bloody discipline that turned them into wage-labourers, the disgraceful action of the state which employed the police to accelerate the accumulation of capital by increasing the degree of exploitation of labour, the question remains: whence came the capitalists originally? For the expropriation of the agricultural population creates, directly, none but great landed proprietors. As far, however, as concerns the genesis of the farmer—it is a slow process evolving through many centuries. The serfs, as well as the free small proprietors, held land under very different tenures, and were therefore emancipated under very different economic conditions. In England the first form of the farmer is the bailiff, himself a serf. His position is similar to that of the old Roman *villicus*, only in a more limited sphere of action. During the second half of the 14th century he is replaced by a farmer, whom the landlord provides with seed, cattle and implements. His condition is not very different from that of the peasant. Only he exploits more wage-labour. Soon he becomes a metayer, a half farmer. He advances one part of the agricultural stock, the landlord the other. The two divide the total product in proportions determined by contract. This form quickly disappears in England, to give place to the farmer proper, who makes his own capital breed by employing wage-labourers, and pays a part of the surplus-product, in money or in kind, to the landlord as rent. So long, during the 15th century, as the independent peasant and the farm-labourer working for himself as well as for wages, enriched themselves by their own labour, the circumstances of the farmer, and his field of production, were equally mediocre. The agricultural revolution which commenced in the last third of the 15th century, and continued during almost the whole of the 16th (excepting, however, its last decade), enriched him just as speedily as it impoverished the mass of the agricultural people.[1]

The usurpation of the common lands allowed him to augment greatly his stock of cattle, almost without cost they yielded him a richer supply of manure for the tillage of the soil. To this, was added in the 16th century, a very important element. At that time the contracts for farms ran for a long time, often for 99 years. The progressive fall in the value of the precious metals, and therefore of money, brought the farmers golden fruit. Apart from all the other circumstances discussed above, it lowered wages. A portion of the latter was not now added to the profits of the farm. The continuous rise in the price of the corn, wool, meat, in a word of all agricultural produce, swelled the money capital of the farmer without any action on his part, whilst the rent he paid (being calculated on the old value of money) diminished in reality.[2] Thus they grew rich at the expense both of their labourers and their landlords. No wonder therefore, that England, at the end of the 16th century, had a class of capitalist farmers, rich, considering the circumstances of the time.[3]

Karl Marx, *Capital*, Vol. 1, Moscow:
Progress Publishers, 1965, pp. 743-744

NOTES

1. Harrison in his "Description of England," says: "Although peradventure foure pounds of old rent be improved to fortie, toward the end of his term, if he have not six or seven yeares rent lieng by him, fiftie or a hundred pounds, yet will the farmer thinke his gaines verie small."

2. On the influence of the depreciation of money in the 16th century, on the different classes of society, see "A Compendious or Briefe Examination of Certayne Ordinary Complaints of Divers of Our Countrymen in These Our Days." By W.S. Gentleman. (London 1581.) The dialogue form of this work led people for a long time to ascribe it to Shakespeare, and even in 1751, it was published under his name. Its author is William Stafford. In one place the knight reasons as follows: Knight: You, my neighbour, the husbandman, you Maister Mercer, and you Goodman Cooper, with other artirficers, may save yourselves metely well. For as much as all things are dearer than they were, so much do you arise in the pryce of your wares and occupations that ye sell agayne. But we have nothing to sell whereby we might advance ye price there of, to countervaile those things that we must buy agayne." In another place the knight asks the doctor: "I pray you, what be those sorts that ye meane? And first, of those that ye thinke should have no losse thereby?—Doctor: I mean all those that live by buying and selling, for as they buy deare, they sell thereafter. Knight: What is the next sort they ye say would win by it? Doctor: Marry, all such as have taing of fearmes in their owne manurance [cultivation] at the old rent, for where they pay after the olde rate they sell after the newe—that is, they paye for theire lande good cheape, and sell all things growing thereof deare. Knight: What sorte is that which, ye sayde should have greater losse hereby, than these men had profit? Doctor: It is all noblemen, gentlemen, and all other that live either by a stinted rent or stipend, or do not manure [cultivation] the ground, or doe occupy no buying and selling.
3. In France, the regisseur, steward, collector of dues for the feudal lords during the earlier part of the middle ages, soon became an homme d'affaires. who by extortion, cheating, etc., swindled himself into a capitalist. These regisseurs themselves were sometimes noblemen. ... Already it is evident here how in all spheres of social life the lion's share falls to the middleman. In the economic domain, e.g. financiers, stock-exchange speculators, merchants, shopkeepers skim the cream; in civil matters, the lawyer fleeces his clients, in politics the representative is of more importance than the voters, the minister than the sovereign; in

religion God is pushed into the background by the "Mediator", and the latter again is shoved back by the priests, the inevitable middlemen between the good shepherd and his sheep. In France, as in England, the great feudal territories were divided into innumerable small homesteads, but under conditions incomparably more unfavourable for the people. During the 14th century arose the farms or terriers. Their number grew constantly, far beyond 100,000. They paid rents varying from 1/12 to 1/5 of the product in money or kind. These farms were fiefs, sub-fiefs, etc., according to the value and extent of the domains, many of them only containing a few acres. But these farmers had rights of jurisdiction in some degree over the dwellers on the soil; there were four grades. The oppression of the agricultural population under all these petty tyrants will be understood. Monteil says that there were once in France 160,000 judges, where today, 4,000 tribunals, including justices of the peace, suffice.

4

Peasant Question in France and Germany

[Friedrich Engels]

Engels wrote this piece in 1894 as a perspective paper for the French and German Social Democratic Parties that were contemplating addressing the plight of small peasants in their election manifesto, and to forge an alliance of workers and peasants. It was a rebuttal of various French Socialists like Vollmar and the agrarian programme adopted in Marseilles in 1892 and supplemented in Nantes in 1894 (Frankfurt Congress of German Social-Democrats). Engels clearly takes a view that small peasants (or for that matter even big peasants), cannot survive the intense competitive pressures of capitalism that pushes them into indebtedness and pauperization. He suggested that the Party should organize them into cooperatives and eventually convince them for nationalization of their landed property but never collectivize the property forcefully.

The bourgeois and reactionary parties greatly wonder why everywhere among Socialists the peasant question has now suddenly been placed upon the order of the day. What they should be wondering at, by rights, is that this has not been done long ago. From Ireland to Sicily, from Andalusia to Russia, and Bulgaria, the peasant is a very essential factor of the population, production and political power. Only two regions of Western Europe form an exception. In Great Britain proper, big, landed estates and large-scale agriculture have totally displaced the self-supporting peasant;

in Prussia east of the Elbe, the same process has been going on for centuries; here, too, the peasant is being increasingly "turned out", or at least economically and politically forced into the background.

The reclusive and disengaged peasant life with respect to national politics makes way for various kinds of parliamentary corruption from Roman times to present-day Paris or Russian despotic rule. Since the rise of the working-class movement in Western Europe, the bourgeois succeeded in creating suspicion of the socialist workers in the minds of the peasants. Socialists are blamed as people who want to "divide up", as lazy, greedy, city dwellers who have an eye on the property of the peasants. The hazy socialist aspirations of the February 1848 Paris Commune were rapidly disposed of by the reactionary ballots of the French peasantry. The peasant, who wanted peace of mind, lost in the legacy of Napoleon, bandied as the emperor of the peasants, and created the Second Empire. We all know what this one false step of the peasants cost the people of France; it is still suffering from its aftermath.

But much has changed since then. The development of the capitalist form of production has cut the life-strings of small production in agriculture; small production is irretrievably going to rack and ruin. Competitors in North and South America and in India have swamped the European market with their cheap grain, so cheap that no domestic producer can compete with it. The big landowners and small peasants alike can see ruin staring them in the face. And since they are both owners of land and country folk, the big landowners assume the role of champions of the interests of the small peasants, and the small peasants by and large accept them as such.

Meanwhile, a powerful socialist workers' party has sprung up and developed in the West, which is able to push obscure social and political presentiments to the background and the broader and deeper scope of a programme to meet all scientific requirements of society. The presence of Social Democratic parties is steadily growing in the German, French, and Belgian parliaments. The conquest of political power that began in towns should go to the country. This party has the capacity to have a clear insight into the interconnections between economic causes and political effects and long ago perceived the big landowner–the wolf in the sheep's clothing, who try to champion the peasant cause. Hope this party may not leave the doomed peasant in the hands of his false protectors who shall turn this passive member into an active opponent of the industrial worker. This brings us right into the thick of the peasant question.

The rural population in which we can address ourselves consists of quite different parts, which vary greatly with the various regions. In the west of Germany, as in France and Belgium, there prevails the small-scale cultivation of small-holding peasants, the majority of whom own and the minority of whom rent their parcels of land. In the northwest–in Lower Saxony and Schleswig-Holstein–we have a preponderance of big and middle peasants who cannot do without male and female farm servants and even day labourers. The same is true of part of Bavaria. In Prussia east of the Elbe, and in Mecklenburg, we have the regions of big landed estates and large-scale cultivation with hinds, cotters, and day labourers, and in between small and middle peasants in relatively unimportant and steadily decreasing proportion. In central Germany, all these forms of production and ownership are found mixed in various proportions, depending upon the locality, without the decided prevalence of any particular form over a large area.

Besides, there are localities varying in extent where the arable land owned or rented is insufficient to provide for the subsistence of the family, but can serve only as the basis for operating a domestic industry and enabling the latter to pay the otherwise incomprehensibly low wages that ensure the steady sale of its products despite all foreign competition. Which of these subdivisions of the rural population can be won over by the Social-Democratic Party?

By small peasant we mean here the owners or tenant–particularly the former–of a patch of land no bigger, as a rule, than he and his family can till, and no smaller than can sustain the family. This small peasant, just like the small handicraftsman, is therefore a toiler who differs from the modern proletarian in that he still possesses his instruments of labour; hence, a survival of a past mode of production. There is a threefold difference between him and his ancestor, the serf, bondsman, or, quite exceptionally, the free peasant liable to rent or sell and feudal services. First, in that the French Revolution freed him from feudal services and dues that he owed to the landlord and, in the majority of cases, at least on the left bank of the Rhine, assigned his peasant farm to him as his own free property.

Secondly, in the post-revolution France, the dismantling of the Mark community system[1] not only granted the freedom for the small peasant but at the same time cut loose from the patronage benefits. This deprives the small peasant the possibility of feeding his draft animals without buying fodder. The number of peasants unable to keep draft animals of their own is steadily increasing. Economically, however, the loss of the emoluments derived from the Mark by far outweighs the benefits accruing from the abolition of feudal services.

Thirdly, the peasant of today has lost half of his former productive activity. Formerly, he and his family produced, from raw material he had made himself, the greater part of the industrial products that he needed; the rest of what he required was supplied by village neighbours who plied a trade in addition to farming and were paid mostly in articles of exchange or in reciprocal services. The family, and still more the village, was self-sufficient, produced almost everything it needed. It was natural economy almost unalloyed; almost no money was necessary. Capitalist production put an end to this by its money economy and large-scale industry. But if the Mark emoluments represented one of the basic conditions of his existence, his industrial sideline was another. And thus the peasant sinks ever lower. Taxes, crop failures, divisions of inheritance and litigations drive one peasant after another into the arms of the usurer; the indebtedness becomes more and more general and steadily increases in amount in each case–in brief, our small peasant, like every other survival of a past mode of production, is hopelessly doomed. He is a future proletarian.

As such, he needs to listen to the socialist programme. But he is prevented from doing so by the culture of petty bourgeois prejudice. With no real friends, it is even more difficult for him to defend his endangered patch of land, the more desperately he clings to it the more he regards the Social-Democrats, who speak of transferring landed property to the whole of society, as just as dangerous a foe as the usurer and the lawyer. How can Social-Democracy overcome this prejudice? What can it offer to the doomed small peasant without becoming untrue to itself? Here we find a practical point of support in the agrarian programme of the French Socialists of the Marxian trend, a programme which is more noteworthy as it comes from the classical land of small-peasant economy.

The Marseilles Congress of 1892 adopted the first agrarian programme of the Party. It demands on behalf of property-less rural workers (that is to say, day labourers and hinds): minimum wages fixed by trade unions and community councils; rural trade courts consisting half of workers; prohibition of the sale of common lands; and the leasing of public domain lands to communities which are to rent all this land, whether owned by them or rented, to associations of propertyless families of farm labourers for common cultivation, on conditions that the employment of wage-workers be prohibited and that the communities exercise control; old-age and invalid pensions, to be defrayed by means of a special tax on big landed estates.

For the small peasants, with special consideration for tenant farmers, purchase of machinery by the community to be leased at cost price to the peasants; the formation of peasant cooperatives for the purchase of manure, drain-pipes, seed, etc., and for the sale of the produce; abolition of the real estate transfer tax if the value involved does not exceed 5,000 francs; arbitration commissions of the Irish pattern to reduce exorbitant rentals and compensate quitting tenant farmers and sharecroppers (me'tayers) for appreciation of the land due to them; repeal of Article 2102 of the Civil Code which allows a landlord to on the distraint crop, and the abolition of the right of creditors to levy on growing crops; exemption from levy and distraint of a definite amount of farm implements and of the crop, seed, manure, draft animals, in short, whatever is indispensable to the peasant for carrying on his business; revision of the general cadastre, which has long been out of date, and until such time a local revision in each community; lastly, free instruction in farming, and agricultural experimental stations.

Part of the proposed programme has already been realized elsewhere. The tenants' arbitration courts follow the Irish prototype by express mention. Peasant cooperatives already exist in the Rhine provinces. The revision of the cadaster (land record system) has been a constant pious wish of all liberals, and even bureaucrats, throughout Western Europe.

The Party did such a good business with this programme among the peasants in the most diverse parts of France. It was felt, however, that this would be treading on dangerous ground. How was the peasant to be helped–as a future proletarian or a present propertied peasant? To decide we need certain conceptual clarity, particularly when the capitalist system is inevitably destroying its mode of production. Let us now examine more closely the demands made in the preamble adopted by the Nantes Congress in September of this year.

The preamble begins as follows:

- Producers can be free only in so far as they are in possession of the means of production.
- While industry attained a degree of capitalist centralization, that they can be restored to the actual producers in the collective social form; but in the sphere of agriculture–at least in present-day France, for lack of such centralization, land is still in the hands of the individual possession.
- In this state of affairs characterized by small-holding ownership is irretrievably doomed, it is not for socialism to hasten its doom, as its task does not consist in separating property from labour. But, on the contrary, lies in uniting both these factors of production by placing them in the same hands; the separation would produce servitude and poverty of the workers when reduced to proletarians.

- The duty of socialism is to put the agricultural proletarians again in possession–collective or social in form, not merely in the maintenance of present small patches of land as against the fisk, the usurer, and the encroachments of the newly-arisen big landowners.
- It is expedient to extend this protection also to tenants or sharecroppers (me'tayers) who may exploit day labourers, but are compelled to do so to a certain extent because of the exploitation to which they themselves are subjected.
- Therefore the Workers' Party which unlike the anarchists, does not count on an increase and spread of poverty for the transformation of the social order but expects labour and society in general to be emancipated only by the organization and concerted efforts of the workers of both country and town, by their taking possession of the government and legislation. It has to adopt an agrarian programme to bring together all the elements of rural production and use the national soil, to wage an identical struggle against the feudality of landownership.

Now, let's examine closely the premises of these goals.

The common possession of the means of production should be the sole principal goal for industry as well as agriculture. According to the programme, individual possession never and nowhere obtained generally for all producers; for that very reason, and because industrial progress removes it anyhow, socialism is not interested in maintaining but rather in removing it; because where it exists and in so far as it exists it makes common possession impossible.

Mere possession of the means of production by the individuals does not grant any real freedom under the capitalist market mechanism. Handicraft has already been ruined in the cities; in metropolises like London. It has already been superseded by large-scale industry, by organizing labour in sweatshops and miserable poor. The self-supporting small peasant is neither in the safe possession of his tiny patch of land, nor is he free. He, as well as his house, his farmstead, and his new fields, belong to the usurer; his livelihood is more uncertain than that of the proletarian, who at least does have tranquil days now and then, which is never the case with the eternally tortured debt slave. Strike out Article 2102 of the Civil Code, provide by law that a definite amount of a peasant's farm implements, cattle, etc., shall be exempt from levy and tax; yet you cannot ensure him against a distress sale of his cattle "voluntarily", in which he must sign himself away, body and soul, to the usurer and be glad to get a reprieve. Your attempt to protect the small peasant in his property does not protect his liberty but only the particular form of his servitude; it prolongs a situation in which he can neither live nor die. It is, therefore, entirely out of place here to cite the first paragraph of your programme as authority for your contention.

The preamble notes that in present-day France, land–the means of production, largely still is in the hands of small and individual producers. However, the task of socialism is not to separate property from labour, for the heck of it, but, on the contrary, is to unite the two by placing them in the same hands. Its task is to transfer the means of production to the producers as their common possession. If we lose sight of this, the above statement becomes directly misleading in that it implies that it is the mission of socialism to convert the present sham property of the small peasant in his fields into real property–that is to say, to convert the small tenant into an owner and the indebted owner into a debtless owner. Undoubtedly, socialism is interested to see that the false semblance of peasant property should disappear, but not in this manner.

At any rate, we have now got so far that the preamble can straightforwardly declare it to be the duty of socialism, indeed, its imperative duty, "to maintain the peasants themselves tilling their patches of land in possession of the same as against the fisk, the usurer and the encroachments of the newly-arisen big landowners."

The preamble thus imposes upon socialism the imperative duty to carry out something which it had declared to be impossible in the preceding paragraph. It charges it to "maintain" the small-holding ownership of the peasants although it itself states that this form of ownership is "irretrievably doomed". What are the fisk, the usurer, and the newly-arisen big landowners if not the instruments by means of which capitalist production brings about this inevitable doom? What means "socialism" is to employ to protect the peasant against this trinity, we shall see below.

It is likewise "expedient to extend this protection also to the producers who, as tenants or sharecroppers (Metayers), cultivate the land owned by others and who, if they exploit day labourers, are to a certain extent compelled to do so because of the exploitation to which they themselves are subjected."

Here, we are entering upon ground that is passing strange. Socialism is particularly opposed to the exploitation of wage labour. And here it is declared to be the imperative duty of socialism to protect the French tenants when they "exploit day labourers", as the text literally states! And that because they are compelled to do so by a certain "exploitation to which they themselves are subjected"!

How easy and pleasant it is to keep on coasting once you are on the toboggan slide! When now the big and middle peasants of Germany come to ask the French Socialists to intercede with the German Party Executive to get the German Social-Democratic Party to protect them in the exploitation of their male and female farm servants, citing in support of the contention the "exploitation to which they themselves are subjected" by usurers, tax collectors, grain speculators and cattle dealers, what will they answer? What guarantee have they that our agrarian big landlords will not send them Count Kanitz (as he also submitted a proposal like theirs, providing for a state monopoly of grain importation) and likewise ask for socialist protection of their exploitation of the rural workers, citing in support "the exploitation to which they themselves are subjected" by stock-jobbers, moneylenders, and grain speculators?

Let us say here, at the outset, that the intentions of our French friends are not as bad as one would suppose. They may have to address even a special case like in Northern France, just as in our sugar-beet districts, land is leased to the peasants subject to the obligation to cultivate beets, on conditions which are extremely onerous. They must deliver the beets to a state factory at a price fixed by it, must buy definite seed, use a fixed quantity of prescribed fertilizer, and on delivery are badly cheated into the bargain. We know all about this in Germany, as well. But if this sort of peasant is to be taken under one's wing, this must be said openly and expressly. If the programme is to cover every case, it may lose the fundamental principle of socialism.

The preamble also talks of 'bringing together all elements of rural production to wage a struggle against the common enemy, i.e. 'the feudal landowner'. But I flatly deny that the socialist workers' party of any country is charged with the task of taking into its fold, in addition to the rural proletarians and the small peasants, also the idle and big peasants and perhaps even the tenants of the big estates, the capitalist cattle breeders and other capitalist exploiters of the national soil. To all of them, the feudality of landownership may appear to be a common foe. On certain questions, we may make common cause with them and be able to fight side by side with them for definite aims. We can use in our Party individuals from every class of society, but have no use whatever for any groups representing capitalist, middle-bourgeois, or middle-peasant interests.

The programme has several demands which are all not in the interests of small peasants. A single progressive tax over and above 3,000 francs, abolished of land tax for small peasants, subsidized farming machinery, lowering of transport charges, or subsidizing fertilizers are all fine, even if some of them benefit mostly large farmers. But such demands gives false comfort about small peasantry. In brief, after the tremendous theoretical effort exhibited in the preamble, the practical proposals of the new agrarian programme are even more unrevealing as to the way in which the French Workers' Party expects to be able to maintain the small peasants in possession of their small holdings, which, on its own territory, are irretrievably doomed.

On one point our French comrades are absolutely right: No lasting revolutionary transformation is possible in France against the will of the small peasant. Only, it seems to me, they have not got the right leverage if they mean to bring the peasant under their influence. They appear to be making risky assurances based on hasty theoretical considerations, in desperation to win the elections.

Let us say it outright: can we win the small peasants by protecting their properties against the rising tide of indebtedness and pauperization? Can we transform the tenant into an owner-cultivator by paying off his debts? Even if we do so, as a small petty producer, can he survive further? It is improper to show short-term improvement in the face of impending long-term disaster. It is not in the interest of the Party to perpetuate the petty bourgeois expectations of small peasants on property rights, which is no different than that of small handicraftsman's desire to become a master. What, then, is our attitude towards the small peasantry? How shall we have to deal with it on the day of our accession to power?

To begin with, the French programme is absolutely correct in stating: that we foresee the inevitable doom of the small peasant, but that it is not our mission to hasten it by any interference or otherwise on our part. Secondly, even when the Party comes to power, it should not forcibly expropriate the small peasants, even by some compensation. One should try organizing them into cooperatives, show the limits of private enterprise, so that he realizes the inevitability of socialization.

Almost 20 years ago, the Danish Socialists, which had only one city, with a large countryside filled with many small farms, were pooling them into a single big farm, reap the benefits of scale, finance, cost saving and better management. By leasing land of the big, additional employment can be created. Peasant cooperatives can further be integrated with industry, generate synergy, transform the cooperatives technologically, and distribute the dividends, raise consciousness entitlements and duties of members to run them with a cooperative spirit.

Individual small farming is what spells their doom, if they insist to continue, large-scale farming would swallow it. In their own interest it is imperative to form a collective. While forming them into a collective is inescapable, they should never be threatened or compelled to give up their holdings. Under the capitalist mode of production, foul play of the state is seldom apparent. The Social Democratic Party, however, should unambiguously back the small peasants and facilitate the cooperatives, even when the process is protracted. This saves the small peasant from falling victim to capitalist penetration, makes him our natural ally in the eventual political action, as prolitarianization is completed in other sectors.

The cost of this reorganization should be made from the state exchequer, since it is an excellent investment for the social reorganization.

We now come to the bigger peasants. Here as a result of the division of inheritance as well as indebtedness and forced sales of land we find a variegated pattern of intermediate stages, from small-holding peasant to big peasant proprietor. Where the middle lives among small-holding peasants, using more of his family labour, his situation will not differ greatly from theirs. But where middle and big peasants predominate and the operation of the farms requires, generally, with farm servants, it is quite a different matter. Of course a workers' party has to fight, in the first place, on behalf of the wage-workers–that is, for the male and female servantry and the day labourers. It is unquestionably forbidden to make any promises to the peasants which include the continuance of the wage slavery of the workers. But, as long as the big and middle peasants continue to exist, as such they cannot manage without wage-workers. If it would, therefore, be downright folly on our part to hold out prospects to the small, middle and big peasants alike.

We have here again the parallel case of the handicraftsmen in the cities. True, they are more ruined than the peasants, some of them still make apprentices do all the work. Many of them realized that their mode of production is inevitably doomed, are coming over. The same applies to the big and middle peasants who likewise inevitably face competition of capitalist production, and the cheap overseas corn, and the growing indebtedness. We can do nothing against this decay except recommend here too the pooling of farms to form cooperative enterprises, in which the exploitation of wage labour will be eliminated more and more, and their gradual transformation into branches of the great national producers' cooperative with each branch enjoying equal rights and duties can be instituted. If they don't listen, they can be left to their fate.

Only the big landed estates present a perfectly simple case. Their land has to be expropriated and nationalized, with or without paying compensation, which depends on the question how we get into power. The bottom line is that the land has to be obtained at the cheapest price.

Thus, we would create the possibilities of socialist production for rural proletarians no sooner than for the urban, and of only a very short time, before we win over to our side the rural workers of Prussia east of the Elbe. But once we have the East-Elbe rural workers, a different wind will blow at once all over Germany. The actual semi-servitude of the East-Elbe rural workers is the main political constituuency of Prussian Junker dominance and overlordship in Germany. In fact, even Junkers are facing the ruination from the competition, as a reaction they are becoming bigots, haughty, supporters of militaristic nationalism of the Reich. Even though they own distilleries and beet-sugar refineries, they are scattered and are failing to muster protection. In spite of state assistance, they are unable to save their economic slide. The semi-serfdom sanctioned by law and custom making unlimited exploitation of the rural workers possible to barely keep the drowning Junkers above water. Sow the seed of Social-Democracy among these workers, give them the courage and cohesion to insist upon their rights, and the glory of the Junkers will be put to an end. The great reactionary power, which to Germany represents the same barbarous, predatory element as Russian tsardom does to the whole of Europe, will collapse like a pricked bubble. The "picked regiments" of the Prussian army will become Social-Democratic, which will result in a shift of power that is pregnant with an entire upheaval. But, for this reason, it is of vastly greater importance to win the rural proletariat east of the Elbe than the small peasants of Western Germany. We shall win it nevertheless.

NOTE

1. The mark system is a social organization that rests on the common tenure and common cultivation of the land by small groups of freemen. Both politically and economically the mark was an independent community, and its earliest members were doubtless blood relatives. In its origin the word is the same as mark or march, a boundary. (Wikipedia - Mark System https://en.wikipedia.org/wiki/Mark_system)

5

The Agrarian Question

[Karl Kautsky]

Karl Kautsky was an outstanding leader of the Social Democratic Party in Germany during 1880-1910, whose Die Agrifrage (The Agrarian Question) published in 1899, was hailed by Lenin as a significant work on the question of small peasants. Kautsky's assessment of the survival of peasant production alongside capitalist production, instead of the presumed decimation under growth of capitalist relations of production in agriculture, presented a programmatic challenge before the social democrats to evolve a worker-peasant alliance. He saw the continuation of peasantry which is totally subsumed under the capitalist mode of production. Kautsky fell out of favour after he opposed the October Revolution and was largely forgotten for a very long time till his work was rediscovered in the 1980s. His work is now being considered extremely useful to understand the agrarian question worldwide. We present a summary of the central argument of his book which is useful for the Indian debate on the agrarian question.

Marx's method of understanding the agrarian question is not how the big farmers would swallow the small nor to ask whether small landholders have a future. Rather, it has to consider all the changes through which agriculture has passed over the course of the capitalist mode of production, how capital is seizing hold of agriculture, revolutionizing it, making old forms of production and property untenable and creating the necessity of new ones.

Peasant and Decline of the Feudal Period

[A] medieval peasant household was a self-sufficient entity not only in producing the output but also in the means of reproduction. What happened in the markets impinged only on the farmer's comforts and luxuries, but not his existence. This self-sufficient and cooperative household, previously indestructible, now became subject to market upheavals. With the development of towns and commercialization, this peasant's life changed. Growth of unknown destinations for the agricultural commodities brought new opportunities that lured the peasant. Yet, direct sale to the final consumer became ever more difficult with the increasing 'commodity' character of agricultural production. Merchants who mediated gained far more leverage to manipulate and took advantage. Dealers in grain and cattle were soon joined by the usurer.

Market uncertainty added to the weather uncertainty that made mayhem of markets. Increasing availability of consumption and production loans, not available till now, turned into instruments of integration of peasants into a new system. The commodities of urban industry that reached the village also sowed the seeds of dissolution of the traditional peasant family. With growing dependence on markets, and cash needs, but with no availability of surplus land, the peasant household had to reduce its size by pushing out members to work outside its farm. The peasant farm is then cut to the minimum, managed mostly by the family labour. Once farming yields to the logic of surplus, the only saleable commodity that remains is labour power. The peasants now work for large farms. Small farms jostle with large farms, and struggle to survive rather than lose the small parcel of land. Development of capitalist production in towns would speed up or accelerate the transformation of the peasant life in the village.

Modern Agriculture

The contribution of modern science and industrialization since the mid-19th century in changing agriculture has been remarkable. The introduction of deep ploughing after the arrival of steam ploughs and electrical ploughs, knowledge of microorganisms (with the invention of the microscope), discovery and use of fertilizers, increased knowledge of soil nature, have all tremendously increased the productivity in agriculture. Intensive cultivation has almost replaced extensive cultivation thereby overcoming the land constraint in increasing production. The development of soil, chemical, botanical, veterinary and agricultural sciences in Europe have unleashed productivity in agriculture, which in turn demanded investment in infrastructure, machinery and adoption of new practices in farm management. The growth of engineering and metallurgical sciences and invention of the steam engine transformed transport that reduced not only human drudgery but also the labour cost besides saving time. A sector that was devoid of any progress for centuries suddenly became a revolutionary branch of modern industry. Agricultural sciences were introduced as a vocational course. Agriculture was completely transformed, not merely in the sense of being more productive, it turned into an enterprise of conserving costs and increasing profits.

Capitalist Character of Agriculture

This modern agriculture cannot exist without money, capital and the generalized character of commodity production. Law of value, which decides the relative value and price through competition, gets established gradually. This does not of course suggest that prices would necessarily reflect the value of the commodity or labour embodied. While it is the use value that should determine the value on any good, it is the exchange value that determines the value in practice. The exchange value is determined by both relative demand for the commodity as well as the extent of labour involved, i.e. the cost of production, the necessary condition of determining the value of any good. However, the price which is the market device to reflect the value need not conform to the latter. The price can deviate from the value, even falling below the cost of production, if the supply overshoots the demand. This dichotomous tendency of price and value under capitalist economy is the fundamental route/ basis of translating surplus value into money value.

Markets existed for centuries in history. Those markets were based on simple commodity production, which involved direct interaction of producers and consumers facing each other. Such markets existed in conjunction with feudalism, guilds, etc. The capitalist commodity production which superseded the simple commodity production is at its culmination point. Workers, who were erstwhile producers, are now alienated from means of production, and become available for surplus value to be expropriated. The involvement of this intermediary who/that now links the value and the price led to the obscuring of the law of value. The now universally operative price, distorts the value by modifying its operation.

Just as Marx explained, the price determined by the market does not necessarily conform to the value of the commodity, a distortion that indeed helps the capitalist to convert the surplus value into profit. The price of an agricultural commodity, in fact should be comprised of three components: wage, rent and profit. It is usually to be set by the least productive farm, owing to higher cost of production. However, under competitive conditions and excess supply, the market determined price tends to erode the profit and even to non-recovery of cost of production. Agricultural markets pose this risk too often due to the specifically unpredictable nature of agricultural production which depends on weather, pests, etc. Even though such a risk is equally faced by the large and small peasantry, the ability of the latter to receive the shock is limited. The position of tenant farmers is even more vulnerable. The capitalist owner-cultivator is cushioned by higher surplus that includes absolute rent (which is retained) in addition to surplus extracted from labour. Still the price that crashes in the agricultural output market may erode these advantages.

The agricultural capitalist enjoys profit from sources other than surplus labour, which is the ground rent, except when he is a tenant. Ground rent involves two components, absolute rent and differential rent. Absolute rent is determined by the least productive land and differential rent determined by relative levels of productivity of the remaining lands. As the demand for food rises, the ground rent is likely to rise. Unlike the machinery which needs replacement, land is not a kind of capital which has a replacement cost. Hence, rent simply accrues to the landlord due to the property right alone rather than for any contribution. The capitalist farmer, who also owns the land enjoys a profit which involves the surplus value plus the ground rent built into the price.

Technical Superiority of Large Farms Over Small Farms

Feudal lords previously cultivated their own lands using human and animal labour with their servile peasant labour, making few improvements to the land. The arrival of capitalist agriculture changes this very structure. The same peasants now become proletarians; the farms now produce for market with a view to earn profit, and farm owners adopt modern means to optimize costs and increase productivity.

Large size farms have several advantages over the small farms in this regard. First, large farms have a greater share of cultivated area than small farms, for having lesser land lost in fencing, boundaries and bunding. Second, they can afford deployment of modern agricultural machinery like steam ploughs, reapers, seed drills, threshers, horse-drawn ploughs and transport carriages compared to small farms. Use of machinery not only increases the quality of operation but saves time which is a critical factor in farming. Third, with increased educational training in agricultural sciences, large farms would employ technically qualified farm managers, who have the necessary knowledge to change the cropping pattern according to changing demand conditions, use appropriate farm management practices, optimize costs and increase productivity. Fourth, modern management of large farms allows better planning, operational efficiency, scale economy, book-keeping, and meticulous cost monitoring. Compared to these advantages, a small peasant holding may be economically more efficient at a micro scale. But the size of the large farm reduces the average cost of overheads, and increases the profits proportionately, making them superior to the small farms. Finally, access to the banking system and larger savings make large farms undertake high risk investments.

Overwork and Under Consumption of Small Farmers

Small farmers have two weapons set against the large farms. First, they provide industrious care in farming, i.e. they spare no effort in exploiting themselves to the utmost. Second, as the fragility of the small independent peasant is ever greater than even that of agricultural labour, the small peasants not only flog themselves into this drudgery, but their family members too. Everyone has to share the yoke as there is no distinction between the farm and the household, which includes men, women, sons, daughters and even old people. They subject their own children to utmost harsh labour. Except culturally imposed holidays, every day is a working day for them. The demand for an eight-hour day appears quite modest in comparison.

Overwork begins once labour for the producer's immediate consumption turns into labour for the market, impelled by the goad of competition. Competing through the lengthening working day goes in tandem with technical backwardness. As an enterprise that cannot fight off competition through technical innovation is forced to resort to imposition of even greater demands on its workers. The possibility of prolonging work time will in turn work as an obstacle to technical progress. Child labour becomes the norm, which undermines their education and capacity to enter skilled labour.

The miserliness of the peasants begins when their farms fall under the sway of competition, denying them even the smallest of pleasures and comforts of life. The small peasant passes the most miserable existence that can ever be imagined. Sometimes, wage labourers are healthier than the small peasant, because he neglects consuming even the minimal diet. The low equilibrium of the anaemic peasant is supported by a malnourished child labour and undernourished old members of the family on demand.

The existence of drudgery also brings its own rewards: the peasant can manage under the most miserable conditions. One has to confess that as far as the subhuman diet of the small peasant is concerned, it is no more an advantage of the small farm than its superhuman industriousness. Both testify to economic backwardness and represent obstacles to economic progress.

The greater care taken by the small peasantry in their work is ruinous for them due to their drudgery and excess frugality. While it is true that workers working for themselves exercise more care towards work than working for others, this is not necessary for a large farm which is equipped with means, capital, technology and organizational capacity. The other weapons of the small farmers' arsenal–over-work, undernourishment and accompanying ignorance offset the effects of the greater care.

The Cooperative System

The cooperative system is of an undeniable importance to the survival of small farmers. But, the question is whether the small farmers see its advantages and agree to it. Even if they agree, how far can the cooperatives survive? Most functional cooperatives are credit cooperatives that operate in allied activities such as dairy and sugar. Mere credit cooperatives have limited benefits. Production cooperatives need lot more coordination among farmers even as they can substantially increase the bargaining power over the price. And the cooperative would benefit farmers only when they are directly involved in running it. The experience is such that large farms are much more keen in forming cooperatives than small farmers, though they benefit. Peasants rarely come together and form cooperatives by themselves, the more proximate reason being lack of trust among themselves and inability to shift to an outside agency over the household.

However, insufficient organizational discipline and lack of democracy in organizing cooperatives would not favour small farms. Large farmers can engage in cooperative activity much more easily than small peasants for a variety of reasons such as, they are relatively few in number who can coordinate well among themselves, and will have the necessary leisure and social capital. The current evidence in Germany and France suggests either gradual or abrupt closure of the cooperatives. There are are very few cooperatives that withstood the test of time. It is not that peasants have not benefited from them. Small peasants, besides lacking skills, also suffer from attitudinal problems like pettiness, lack of mutual trust and cooperative spirit and excessive attachment to their property. Hence, peasants do not naturally come together to try the cooperative alternative between the compelled transition of small farmers to large farms.

Limits of Capitalist Enterprise

In spite of conclusive evidence of the inherent superiority of large farms, we also have to explain the existence and sometimes proliferation of small farms beyond Germany, including those in England, and France. Even bourgeois economists right from Adam Smith and Sismondi have expressed their approval of small farms over hitherto existing latifundiums where tenant farmers precariously existed under duress. In England small farms did not decline, in Germany mid-size farms increased, in France small farms proliferated, during 1840-1890. The number of large farms increased only in the USA, which had a different history. The contradictory statistics indeed suggest that there is no necessary link between the size of the farm and capitalist relations in agriculture. They certainly call for the need for further research. We must understand that even in industry, there is no linear decline or demise of small enterprise. There are always pockets in which small enterprise survived taking advantage of their abilities to survive (p. 144).

Further, unlike in industry, large-scale farming is not always superior in agriculture, which is contingent on nature of crop, relative requirement and availability of mechanization. There are crops that require close and compact monitoring which are better managed by small farmers (p. 148). Similarly, shortage of labour power and high wages can make capitalist farms impossible at times. Before the mechanization solves the labour shortage issue, small farms need the advantage of unpaid family labour to compete in the market.

Large farms can also have a vested interest in keeping small farms alive, which assures them labour supply in the country-side by preventing complete migration of labour. It also keeps the wages in check, small farmers who get part of substance from their farms tend to accept lower wages. It is not uncommon to see large farms to coexist with small farms in several regions.

6

Is Class Struggle the Prime Mover in Transition from Feudalism to Capitalism?[1]

[Stephan R. Epstein]

Rodney Hilton's name is synonymous with the 'prime mover' thesis. He was a founding member of the Historians' Group of the British Communist Party, and the editor of *Past and Present* during 1942-68. Hilton was enormously influential in the pre-1968 Marxist debate in extending Maurice Dobb's thesis that the 'class struggle' between the serfs/peasants and the feudal lords was the 'prime mover' in the transition from feudalism to capitalism. In the essay summarized here Epstein argues that the Dobb/Epstein framework is inadequate to analyse the temporal and spatial dimensions of capitalist transition in Western Europe. Transition to capitalism, Epstein argues, should also be placed in the context of complex political, social and technological changes that led to the undermining of feudalism and development of capitalist forces of production.

How Did Feudalism Begin to Fail in England/Europe?

Epstein begins with a critique of Maurice Dobb's work that had a crucial influence on Hilton and most other British Communist historians. For Dobb feudalism faced a 'general crisis' in England in the 15th century as it was fundamentally an inefficient system that was destined to fail. That failure was caused by systemic disincentives to capital accumulation and technological innovation, and peasant over-exploitation, which in turn gave rise to a class conflict between peasants and feudal lords.

If feudalism is to be characterized as an inefficient mode, Epstein asks, how does one account for its success in expanding territorially, economically and technologically, for more than half a millennium before it is hit by the crisis? We do not find a positive theory of the development of feudalism here. Dobb's reading of pre-capitalist epochs, he argues, was mediated by the theories which argued that feudal societies were scarcity-driven and did not respond positively to price incentives and markets.

The second weakness of Dobb's model, according to Epstein, was its overwhelming focus on English history. There were good reasons for this, including the paradigmatic nature of England in Marx's narrative of the transition to capitalism and the state of historical research at the time Dobb wrote. Confining the transition debate to the English experience helped to mask the difficulties that a strictly Marxist class-based analysis will face in explaining the problematic of uneven development. Two critical questions were never posed. First, why did the transition to capitalism occur first in Western Europe, even though parts of Asia were previously economically more advanced? And, second, why was the English economy between 1400 and 1700 able first to catch up with, and then to forge ahead of, previously more advanced Continental European regions?

Hilton's documentation of rural struggle and resistance against landlord exploitation was crucial in establishing feudalism not as a stable and static social order, but as an unstable social system riven with contradictions. The conflict between peasants and landlords led to the differentiation and transition; eviction of self-sufficient peasants to benefit a class of wealthy peasants who increasingly produced for market. This change generated large numbers of dependent wage earners who had to meet most of their living requirements through the market. For Hilton, Epstein notes, it was ultimately the class struggle that gave rise to agrarian capitalism and competitive, capitalist markets of sellers and buyers. Class struggle was the prime mover, that 'explained' the transition to industrial capitalism. However, Epstein asks if the dispossession of economically self-sufficient peasants from the land is a necessary and sufficient cause for the rise of a technologically dynamic, fully commoditized, capitalist mode of production.

To answer these comparative historical questions, Epstein says, it would be necessary to introduce the two pillars of Marxian analysis that were either weak or missing from (Dobb's and) Hilton's account: a theory of technological development and a political economy of states and markets.

A. For both Dobb and Hilton, Epstein notes, technological progress during feudalism was so primitive that it did not matter. Hilton had argued that the landlords invested at the rate of a mere 5 per cent, which was insufficient to support 13th century productivity. Rather than invest in capital, the lords tended to invest in maintenance of a large retinue and army; to spend most income on personal display; to upkeep their social and political standing. The peasants, burdened by feudal rents, feudal exactions, ecclesiastical tithes, arbitrary royal purveyancing, growing state taxation and land fragmentation, were deprived of the necessary surplus for investment in capital stock. But, Epstein points out that a net annual rate of capital accumulation of 5 per cent in the 13th and 14th centuries is not too low for a preindustrial economy. Hilton's subsequent emphasis on rising land-man ratio caused by the Black Death as leading to class struggle too, is inadequate as an explanation, because, he argues, the land-man ratio was also never stable or consistent due to wars and many other factors. Such endogenous factors did not matter for Hilton.

   What about the exogenous factors? Epstein argues that Dobb and Hilton moved towards acknowledging growth of petty commodity production under feudalism and the active role played by the state in the growth of the institutional framework, although they did not think their model through sufficiently.

B. The second important question was that of the role of trade in feudalism. Was the feudal mode of production primarily a subsistence economy or did they produce for the markets too? Epstein notes that, even though such a possibility of peasant petty commodity production was not acknowledged by Dobb and Hilton (in the 1940s), they had to reconsider that position in the later years, in the face of the overwhelming evidence on monetization of peasant production in the late medieval period. Growing trade enabled production for markets thus offering the producers, 'both the means and the motive for improving cultivation' and for engaging in petty commodity exchange. It led to class differentiation and capital accumulation within the economy of small producers.

C. Third is the role of the state in the growth of institutional framework. Epstein notes that even though these factors were not important for Hilton initially, he did come round to a more positive view of this characteristic feature of feudal society, perhaps influenced by Perry Anderson's Lineages of the Absolutist State (1976) which introduced Weberian definitions of feudalism based on 'jurisdictional fragmentation' into the Marxist canon. Eventually Hilton included three factors linked with decentralized power among European feudalism's five principal characteristics: i) Decentralized power in feudalism as an essential aspect, not a weakness, of feudal society; ii) Landlord power for the purpose of surplus extraction as expressed through private jurisdiction; iii) 'Feudal rent' that included payments for seigneurial monopolies (including, presumably, taxation of trade); iv) Peasant commodity production as central to feudalism and 'provided the bulk of landlord income'; v) Merchant capital and large-scale urbanization denoting 'a further development of this money element in the relations of production'.

Where Do We Go from There?

For Epstein, a theory of the feudal mode of production and of the transition to capitalism requires a clear definition of the historical beginning and end. He defined feudalism as a social-economic formation featuring a prevalence of:

1. Decentralized power to landlords, expressed through private jurisdiction.
2. 'Feudal rent' includes payments for seigneurial monopolies (besides commercial taxes).
3. Centrality of peasant commodity production to the economy and
4. Money element introduced in the relations of production by mercantile capital and urbanization.

For Epstein, any theory of the transition from feudalism to capitalism must, at least, answer the following historical questions:

1. How did agricultural supply keep up with growing population (demand)?
2. Second, how did exclusive property rights develop?
3. How did the wage-based, non-agricultural sector expand, such that the share of population employed in agriculture fell from c. 90-95 per cent at the outset of feudalism (across Europe, c. 1100) to c. 30 per cent as the capitalist socio-economic formation was taking full shape (in England, c. 1800)? and
4. How did technology in the energy and manufacturing sectors progress, as Marx put it, 'out of the hand-mill into the steam-mill'?

Feudalism and Trade: Emergent Contradictions

Epstein draws on the substantial body of research which demonstrated that agricultural supply in medieval and early modern Europe was far more elastic than either Marxists like Hilton or 'Ricardo-Malthusian' pessimists like Postan. The major bottleneck to productivity gains in feudal agriculture was not technological, as Postan claimed, for the best technology of the times was already available to 13th century agriculturalists that was adequate to supply food to a growing population. The most notable feature of feudal agriculture was, by contrast, the astonishing inefficiency with which best practices were applied: feudal political and jurisdictional fragmentation and warfare; resulting failures in coordination; and lack of investment in public goods such as transport and commercial arrangements, credible and predictable justice and financial and political stability.

His method foregrounds the feudal state and society on which economic aspects are seen as dependent. Here property rights are understood to include a broad set of institutional practices that make the right work rather than as a narrow idea of individualized ownership. Such methodological departures enable him to focus on all such conditions that made investment in agriculture profitable, rather than focus on the technical or organizational characteristics of feudal agriculture itself.

Epstein laid out his model of feudalism as follows. In the feudal-tributary mode of production, most rural producers owned their means of production and sold a portion of their produce on the market. Therefore, they responded positively to changes in supply and demand and relative prices. Feudal lords (who included the ruling elites in towns with jurisdictional prerogatives over the hinterland) extracted an agricultural surplus from the peasantry through decentralized legal compulsion backed by military threat; the surplus was extracted directly as rent in cash, kind or labour, and indirectly through taxation, levies on trade and the provision of justice. Although the relative share of income from different sources varied over time and space, the share from rights of jurisdiction (which sometimes also included compulsory labour services) was always substantial. The principal threat to feudalism thus did not come from trade–up to a point feudalism thrived on trade.

He argues that the main obstacle to agricultural growth in the feudal economy was the cost of trade, which was largely defined by institutional regulation and tariffs; by political and military stability; and to a lesser extent by developments in transport technology. The lords' and towns' main purpose in stimulating trade was to maximize rents from their jurisdictional rights. Those rights were a basic feature of their social and political power. As a result, the introduction of jurisdictionally 'free' trade did not just lower feudal and urban revenues–it also challenged the superiority of lord over peasant and town over country.

However, in the longer run, he points out that strong feudal and urban jurisdiction became incompatible with agrarian development. By the later Middle Ages, agricultural innovation was inversely correlated with the intensity of seigneurial rights, and rural proto-industrial growth was inversely correlated with the jurisdictional powers of towns. This brought the heart of feudalism's central contradiction to the fore: the political economy of feudalism was necessary to establish markets and to coordinate economic activities during its first great phase of expansion (c. 950-1250), but already by 1300 that same political economy–which combined market monopolies and the coordination failures arising from political and jurisdictional parcelization–had begun to fetter further growth. So, by 1300, the fundamental constraint on feudal agriculture came from feudal institutional constraints, rather than from technological inertia.

Moreover, Epstein notes that, beneath these overarching features, the political economy of feudal Europe displayed strong diversity. In most of Western Europe, the use of lordly powers of coercion to tax and monopolize trade, which kept the economy substantially below its full agricultural potential, was counterbalanced by the lords' strategy of territorial expansion through localized war. Although the main goal of territorial expansion was to increase the total available political and economic resources, expansion also improved economic efficiency by increasing jurisdictional integration, reducing transaction costs within the new territory, reducing seigniorial dues, weaken or abolish rival feudal and urban monopolies, systematize legal codes and legislation, weights and measures, help coordinate markets and reduce opportunities for pillage and warfare, and restrict rulers' opportunities to act as autocratic 'stationary bandits' against their subjects.

Thus, Epstein notes, gradual political centralization weakened the decentralized mode of economic coercion. Property rights over commercial transactions now got sanctioned by a centralized state-induced economic coercion. From the 15th century, economic aspects began dominating political decision-making. By embarking on the road to centralized, monopolistic jurisdiction, early modern states also laid the institutional bases of modern capitalism and capitalist class struggle.

In sum, Epstein notes, agricultural expansion in the feudal system was the result of two countervailing forces, one pressing for military and jurisdictional decentralization, which made trade and investment more costly, the other is the increased political and jurisdictional centralization, which reduced the costs of investment and trade. In the long run, the latter prevailed, leading to a reduction in transaction costs, stimulating commercialization and specialization. The 'prime mover' and the 'contradiction' within the feudal mode of production lay in the relations between lords, peasants, markets and the state.

Technological Innovation in the Transition to Capitalism

Owing to underdeveloped agricultural and botanical sciences and weather and market risks, technological innovation in agriculture was slow. But Epstein argues that industry could not have experienced a capitalist transition without the technological progress achieved by the pre-modern craftsmen and engineers. In fact, it explains why feudal Europe was able to catch up with and forge ahead of its Eurasian peers.

Epstein tracks technological progress in feudal Europe as follows: such knowledge was largely tacit and experience-based and it was not possible to reproduce it in different places in the absence of codification. Movement of individual experts was quite costly and made transfer of such customary knowledge quite slow under feudalism.

From the late 11th century, however, a distinctive 'feudal' craft-based apprenticeship training through guilds emerged, along with the demand for skilled workers. Membership in these guilds was non-ascriptive which enabled skilled workers to move from city to city with few restrictions or penalties; inter-state competition for technology and high-status consumer goods were held due to which such specialized knowledge could circulate and cross-fertilize; such technicians could move where their skills were most required. The costs of such technical dissemination fell over time in response to growing inter-state competition for skilled workers, and due to urbanization.

Urbanization, especially the development of regional and national metropolises after the late medieval crisis in 15th century, offered improved opportunities for exchange of knowledge; higher average quality of labour, a greater likelihood of matching skills to demand, and stronger incentives for knowledge modelling and codification. Migration of skilled artisans from central and northern Italy (1200-1450), to the southern Rhineland and southern Netherlands (c. 1450-1570), to the Dutch Republic (1570-1675) and finally to Britain after c. 1675 helped to draw on the accumulated knowledge of its predecessors, recombine it with local experience, and develop the knowledge pool further. This gave rise to a sharp, secular increase in the rate of technical innovation and diffusion across Western Europe. A second marked increase in the rate of innovation followed the '17th century crisis', when coordination within states and competition between states increased sharply.

A considerable growth of manufacturing in the urban and countryside since the 14th century resulted in an unusual absorption of labour in proto-industrial activities in England. The rising rural proto-industry threatened traditional urban occupations and the urban tax base, and was frowned upon by town rulers. It also had to be careful not to absorb displaced peasants overnight that could anger the landlords. Gradual alienation of labourers from means of production, which made them footloose, and find employment in the non-agricultural sector eventually undermined feudal coercion.

In conclusion, the underlying, unifying factor of the two great 'feudal crises' of the Marxist canon, is the rate of development of the productive forces.

NOTE

1. Stephan R. Epstein (1960-2007), was a British economic historian, and a professor at the LSE. This is a summary of his paper titled "A Critique of Rodney Hilton: On 'the Prime Mover' in the Transition Debate" published by the Department of Economic History, London School of Economics, 2006, as a working paper (No. 94/06).

REFERENCES

Epstein, S.R., 2007. 'Rodney Hilton, Marxism and the Transition from Feudalism to Capitalism' in C. Dyer, P. Cross, C. Wickham (eds.) Rodney Hilton's *Middle Ages, 400-1600* (Cambridge, 2007).

Dobb, M.H., *Studies in the Development of Capitalism* (London, 1946).

Hilton, R.H. (ed.), *The Transition from Feudalism to Capitalism* (London, 1976), with an 'Introduction' by Hilton. See R.H. Hilton and H. Fagan, *The English Rising of 1381* (London, 1950).

Hilton, R.H., *Bondmen Made Free. Medieval Peasant Movements and the English Rising of 1381* (London, 1973); Hilton, *Class Conflict and the Crisis of Feudalism. Essays in Medieval Social History*, rev. 2nd ed. (London, 1990).

Hilton, R.H., 'Introduction', in T.H. Aston and C.H.E. Philip in (eds.) *The Brenner Debate: Agrarian Class Structure and Economic Development in Pre-Industrial Europe* (Cambridge, 1985).

7

Is Indian Agriculture Feudal, Semi-Feudal or Capitalist?

[Praful Bidwai]

This summary offers insights from the two decade long debate among Indian academics who sought to understand the tendencies in Indian agriculture and determine if it was feudal or if it was moving away from feudalism towards capitalism. Assessing the mode of production was deemed essential to shape the nature of struggle that the Left politics should undertake. Several field studies from many corners of the Indian subcontinent formed the backbone of varying assessments arrived at by participants in the debate.[1] *We chose this review over others (such as Daniel Thorner's) as it takes into account the impact of colonialism and also discusses the political implications of each of the positions taken by the participants. The essay concludes that, given the evidence of growth of capitalist relations of production in agriculture, the orthodox Left should stop fighting the 'phantom of feudalism' and focus on organizing and articulating the interests of the landless labourers and the marginal farmers against capitalist exploitation. This debate forms an important and integral part of the broad Marxist debate on the agrarian question.*

A passionate debate raged for one and a half decades among the Indian and foreign scholars of broadly Marxist persuasion on the mode of production prevalent in Indian agriculture during the 1960s and 70s. The participants included prominent scholars such as Ashok Rudra, Amit Bhaduri, Utsa Patnaik, Jairus Banaji,

John Harriss, Daniel Thorner, Nirmal Chandra, Pradhan Prasad, Hamza Alavi and others. The debate raised a series of questions, such as:

- What are the dominant production relations in Indian agriculture?
- Are they 'pre-capitalist' or 'semi-feudal' or 'capitalist'?
- Are landlordism, sharecropping, tenancy, and rent extraction, and unfree labour necessarily semi-feudal?
- How did colonialism impact agrarian relations and the land property regime?
- Is petty commodity production in agriculture evolving towards capitalism?
- Which is the main line of class conflict and what alliances should the Left forge?

The exchange of ideas between scholars was built on the foundations of the classical debate on transition from feudalism to capitalism between Paul Sweezy, Maurice Dobb, Rodney Hilton, Takahashi and others in the 1950s regarding European and other experiences. Although the participants in the Indian debate were scholars and activists who explored various themes based on evidence and argumentation, its backdrop was provided by radical mobilizations from the late 1960s onwards, including the Naxalbari upsurge in West Bengal, South India and northern states. The debate, although it did not influence the tactics and strategies of various communist parties, did provide the basis at a broader level for the relevance of a protracted agrarian people's war vis-a-vis urban working class mobilization within bourgeois democracy.

The Beginnings

The debate was inaugurated in 1969 by Ashok Rudra with a sample survey of villages in Punjab. He contended that there had been no significant growth of capitalist farming even in this relatively prosperous region. The category of 'capitalist farmers'—who cultivated their lands with higher proportion of hired labour than their own family labour, generated market surplus and used farm machinery and investment–was not statistically significant among the total number of farmers.

Rudra was challenged by Utsa Patnaik on the methodological ground 'of using unhistorical categories'. She argued that the use of wage labour and market surplus were not adequate to define capitalist relations. Equally indispensable were 'capitalist intensification' or accumulation and reinvestment of surplus value on an ever-increasing scale. Ex-colonial countries like India were characterized by a limited and distorted development of capitalism which did not revolutionize the mode of production. She contended that farm size by itself was not an indicator of feudal or capitalist relations; and that private property could exist with functioning land and labour markets without capitalist relations of production. Paresh Chattopadhyay intervened to argue that this was impossible since property relations were only a juridical expression of relations of production.

Indian Agriculture as Semi-Feudal in Nature

In 1956, Daniel Thorner, an American Marxist scholar exiled in India, observed that there were 'built-in depressors' in the production regime in the Indian countryside, generated by a combination of legal, economic and social relations unique to Indian society. Skewed land distribution, tenancy with sharecropping, usurious moneylending, high rents extracted by landlords, poor technological progress, etc. made peasant-cultivators too impoverished. Such 'depressors' ensured agrarian stagnation and low productivity. This argument came to be seen as describing 'semi-feudal' relations in Indian agriculture.

Amit Bhaduri was a prominent exponent of this thesis. After a survey of 20 villages in West Bengal in 1970 he prepared an elegant mathematical model of semi-feudalism: a sharecropping tenant borrows money for production and consumption purposes from *jotedar*–the landlord at an exorbitant rate of interest. The *jotedar* now has twin incomes of rent and interest; the total output of the tenant necessarily falls below this combination of rent and interest; resulting inability to repay keeps the *kisan* in a debt bondage. The landlord can develop a vested interest, not to invest in technology, which may give scope for the tenant to get out of the trap with increased productivity. The semi-feudal landlord becomes the parasite on the producer and the relations of production of the system becomes an obstacle for the growth of production forces in the classic Marxian sense. [Any intervention such as access to formal credit, regulation of rent through tenancy regulation and/or new agricultural technology should logically end semi-feudal relations].

These conclusions were further supported by studies of Pradhan H. Prasad in Bihar and Nirmal Kumar Chandra in West Bengal which also argued that landlords would oppose any new technology and would want to preserve the servile relations, low productivity and under-utilization of resources. All the three concluded that for the period 1951-71 semi-feudal characterization held true for most parts of India.

Such semi-feudal forces were created and consolidated during the colonial rule and later on, Nirmal Chandra pointed out and continued to hold onto the massive labour surplus on a scale that was probably unparalleled in history. Given the extreme weakness of industrial capitalism in India, one could also not envisage any rapid improvement on the industrial front.

Ranjit Sau supplemented Chandra with the argument that small peasants continued to cultivate land despite meagre returns because of lack of alternative opportunities in industry to the point of reducing their own consumption to an unbelievable minimum. Capitalist farmers would face a formidable task of displacing these self-exploiting small tenants.

In a radical shift from his earlier position, Ashok Rudra (1974) criticized Chandra for claiming that there was any such class in West Bengal that resorted to usury and rental income rather than make capital investment in irrigation, fertilizers and new technology. He even gathered micro evidence to demonstrate the trend of concentration of land by large landowners. Rudra wondered why farmers found it hard to find labour during the peak times if there was such a huge surplus labour. Contradicting his own position on

Punjab in 1969, he stated that if generation of surplus value using wage labour and appropriation of surplus through reinvestment amounted to capitalist relations in agriculture, such relations were abundant in West Bengal.

Colonial Mode of Production

Along with understanding of the complex relation between 'observable' phenomena like wage labour, capital formation or size many scholars also focused on the complex juridical, economic and political developments that took shape under the prolonged colonial rule. Crucial were the interventions of scholars like Jairus Banaji, Ashok Rudra, Kathleen Gough, and Gail Omvedt.

Jairus Banaji, to consider one example of the above, took up the issue of the seemingly incompatible coexistence of wage labour and tenant-landlord-moneylender bondage relations, raised by Amit Bhaduri and Utsa Patnaik. He brought in issues of production and realization to explain the latter. Banaji drew attention to a critical distinction made by Marx between the two forms of 'subsumption of labour into capital'. First was the historical process wherein the small producers get incorporated into the supply chain, Marx referred to this as 'formal subsumption'. The second variety is when workers get incorporated into production. This process of appropriation was referred to as 'real' subsumption. The former involved indirect exploitation of surplus value of peasants, while the latter involved direct exploitation.

Yet, Banaji contended that even the formal subsumption of labour into capital implied that the very process of production had become part of the process of capital itself, i.e. of the self-expression of value, of the conversion of money into capital. This in turn implied that capital was here the actual owner of the process of production and the immediate producer was merely a factor in the production process and dependent on the direction of the capitalist. Banaji further argued that without explicit emergence of the capitalist commodity-wage relations at national scale, capitalist relations of exploitation might be widespread. He cited the case of the Deccan during 1850-90, when villages were drawn into production of cotton, sugar, groundnut, and garden crops for growing populations of Bombay and Pune. This led to thorough exploitation of the petty commodity producer through unequal exchange and impoverished the countryside while allowing the cities to accumulate. The pure capitalist nature of the relation between the peasant and moneylender was concealed by the fact that surplus value extorted from the small producer would be called "interest". Banaji held that different forms of tenancy prevalent in India therefore were neither pre-capitalist nor semi-feudal, but were perfectly capitalist. It did not matter if the peasants farmed using a large number of permanent farm labour or used different forms of tenancy as it did not affect the social character or content of production. Similarly, indebtedness as such could not be seen as a hallmark of 'pre-capitalist' relations, because it was precisely through the power of money that the despotism of capital would initially get established.

Hamza Alavi also held a similar perspective. Alavi held that peasant farming continued in India on the basis of largely unchanged techniques. But it was nonetheless subject to formal subsumption of labour by capital through extraction of rent and at a later stage, by 'real' subsumption through direct exploitation of labour under capitalist relations of production. Peasants, he argued, were more resilient than urban petty commodity producers because they need not depend on the market for their food and shelter and desperately held onto their tiny plots of land. But their conditions were progressively undermined by the 'dynamics of peripheral capitalist development'.

Kathleen Gough on the basis of her analysis of Thanjavur district of Tamil Nadu, argued that the capitalist mode of production was dominant for the late 19th to 20th century despite the persistence of certain pre-capitalist features, like giving traditional gifts, caste discrimination, corporal punishments to labour, etc. During 1947-80, Thanjavur district experienced remarkable growth backed by adoption of new technology in hybrid seeds, fertilizers, pesticides, tractors, tube wells, and electric pump sets. She noted a continuous rise in deployment of machinery and other tools (organic composition of capital) particularly among large holdings and the extraction of relative surplus value.

Omvedt and Rudra brought the issue of caste oppression into the discourse, to argue for the need to fight both social oppression and caste exploitation simultaneously. Omvedt held that capitalism was dominant in Indian agriculture now, unlike in pre-independence times, because of: dependence of over half the rural population on wages, generalized commodity production, marketed surplus, means of production in agriculture produced industrially and modern methods of cultivation. In short, the dominant mode of surplus extraction was capitalist.

Rudra made a foray into history to argue that proponents of Indian feudalism like R.S. Sharma or B.N.S. Yadav were comprehensively wrong. He held that the struggle against the reactionary element of Brahmanical ideology should constitute an important element in any struggle for progress in the countryside.

The debate was greatly enriched empirically by a discussion of the rural class structure in its interplay with caste by Mencher, Chandra, Patnaik, Rudra, Prasad, and Bardhan among others. They engaged with issues of labour exploitation, the complex and changing relationship between strata of peasantry, the 'hybridity' of class of big landowners (part feudal, part-capitalist) and the growing or emerging contradictions between the landlords and big peasantry on the one hand and the poor peasantry and landless labour on the other. Further insights were provided by Jan Breman in his work on different forms of labour bondage and their compatibility with capitalism, and the historical analysis of landlordism in Bengal by Rajat Ratna Ray.

Also explored in the discussion was the emergent bonding between different class and caste groups in the Hindi belt; the changing power balance between the traditionally dominant upper castes and the rising middle castes (OBCs), a phenomenon that would soon lead to the 'Forward March of the Backward' and the Mandal scheme of reservations for the OBCs.

The majority opinion here was that the most important contradiction in the countryside was between the big landowners (including the rich peasants) and the labourers (landed or landless)—although there were differences on the role of middle peasant and other issues.

Political Implications of This Debate/ Implications of the Debate for Political Practice

A the end of one and a half decades of the debate, Alice Thorner concluded, "there would no longer appear to be any doubt that capitalism today dominates Indian agriculture as it already was generally seen to dominate industry. Does this mean that the mode of production which prevails in contemporary India is capitalist and subject to the Marxist laws of motion of capitalist development? Here, the answer is less evident, since India's capitalism has emerged in a colonial setting, markedly different from conditions in metropolitan countries where capitalism was born". Yet argues Thorner, "it has been abundantly shown that the existence of widespread tenancy, and/or sharecropping does not necessarily indicate feudal relations of production, nor does concentration of landholding together with cultivation of small units by a large number of peasants. By the same token, the use of wage labour cannot by itself be taken as a sure sign of capitalist relations. Yet, the shift from exploitation through tenants to large-scale or intensive farming by means of hired labour is significant."

Further Thorner argues, "the growth of capitalist farming in India has been accompanied by, in fact amounts to a transformation of relations of production and forms of exploitation. Servile, debt-bonded, and/or traditionally tied labour has been largely supplanted by free, relatively mobile, wage labour, paid in cash. Investment in modern scientific agriculture has enormously expanded, and has resulted on the whole, in enhanced production, at least in certain areas in certain crops. Tenancy and sharecropping arrangements have in many regions been adapted to new economic and technical requirements. Nevertheless, there is agreement that capitalism in agriculture cannot be depended upon to solve the crucial problem of access to land and to food of the whole rural population".

Rudra and Chakravarty reached an important political conclusion that "the orthodox Left standpoint in this country has been that the main enemy of progress in rural areas is feudalism. This gave rise to demand for land to the tiller. Feudalism being the only enemy, the orthodox Left parties have treated, in practice, all remaining classes from rich peasants to landless labour as possible allies. Feudalism in the countryside is considered as regressive and emerging capitalism as progressive. However, tenancy is not necessarily any more feudal or any less capitalistic as in a non-agricultural setting."

Rudra, who started the entire mode of the production debate, had the last word on its political significance. "In the meanwhile, the political interest of landless labourers and poor peasants has gone by default. That is bound to happen whenever attempts are made to build a united front of all non-feudal rural classes against a phantom of feudalism. The orthodox Left parties have thus ended up by supporting the emergent forces of agrarian capitalism to the hilt in the name of fighting feudalism." This comment was doubtless eloquent, and acerbic, even vitriolic. But it drew virtually no response from the 'orthodox' parties at which it was directed.

Four decades later, the understanding of the major Left parties, including the ML, continues to hang onto the 'semi-feudal' character of Indian agriculture and is still focused on either organizing or speaking on behalf of the farmers or peasants as an undifferentiated sector. Despite the large-scale evidence of real subsumption of agriculture into capitalist relations of production, very rarely do we find the interests of the landless labourers and poor peasants being spoken about separately.

NOTE

1. This is the summary of 'The Mode of Production Debate', in the Appendix in the book authored by Praful Bidwai, *The Phoenix Moment: Challenges Confronting the Indian Left*, New Delhi: Harper Collins, 2015.

REFERENCES

Alavi, Hamza, 1981. 'Structure of Colonial Formations', *Economic and Political Weekly*, Vol. 16, No. 10/12, Annual Number (March, 1981).

Banaji, J., 1977. 'Capitalist Domination and the Small Peasantry: Deccan Districts in the Late Nineteenth Century', *Economic and Political Weekly*, 12 (33–4): 1375–404.

Bardhan, P., ed., 1989. *The Economic Theory of Agrarian Institutions*. Oxford: The Clarendon Press.

Bhaduri, A., 1973. 'Agricultural Backwardness Under Semi-Feudalism'. *The Economic Journal*, LXXXIII (329): 120–37.

Chandra, Nirmal, 1975. 'Agrarian Transition in India' *Frontier*, Vol. VII, No. 29, pp. 3-9.

Chattopadhyaya, Paresh, 1972. 'On the Question of Mode of Production in Indian Agriculture: A Further Comment', *Economic and Politial Weekly*, March 25.

Gough, Kathleen, 1980. 'Modes of Production Debate in India', *Economic and Political Weekly*, 16 February.

Hilton, Rodney, 1978. *The Transition from Feudalism to Capitalism*, Verso, London.

Omvedt, Gail, 1981. 'Capitalist Agriculture and Rural Classes in India', *Economic and Political Weekly*, Vol. 16, No. 52 (December 26, 1981), pp. A140-159.

Patnaik, U., 1986. 'The Agrarian Question and Development of Capitalism in India', *Economic and Political Weekly*, 21 (18): 781–93.

Patnaik, U., 1987. *Peasant Class Differentiation: A Study in Method with Reference to Haryana.* New Delhi: Oxford University Press.

Prasad, Pradhan H., 1987. 'Towards a Theory of Transformation of Semi-Feudal Agriculture', *Economic and Political Weekly*, Vol. 22, No. 31 (August 1, 1987).

Rudra, Ashok, 1978. 'Class Relations in Indian Agriculture: I, '*Economic and Political Weekly*, Vol. 13, No. 22 (June 3, 1978), pp. 916-923.

Sweezy, Paul and Maurice Dobb, 1950. 'The Transition from Feudalism to Capitalism', *Science and Society*, Vol. 14, No. 2, 134-67.

Thorner, A., 1982. 'Semi-Feudalism or Capitalism? Contemporary Debate on Classes and Modes of Production in India', Parts 1, 2 and 3. *Economic and Political Weekly*, 17 (49, 50, 51): 1961–8, 1993–9, 2061–86.

8

Three Models of Transition from Feudalism to Capitalism: England, France and Prussia[1]

[Terence J. Byres]

Many political debates take the agrarian transition in England as the sole/exemplary model of European transition from feudalism to capitalism. This then is sought to be applied to countries across the world to assess the extent, degree and nature of agrarian transition, both in academic literature and political activism. I argue that even within Europe, leave alone in the Americas and Asian countries of Japan, South Korea, the agrarian transition has been extremely varied. The essay presents the three examples of England, France and Germany to highlight the complexity of processes that determined and shaped the development of capitalism in agriculture: the institution of full private property rights; the nature of control exercised by the feudal lords over the state; the kind of taxation policy of the state; the demand for agricultural goods; availability of legal recourse for the tenants and peasants to challenge feudal control over their land and labour and other social institutions. While taking snapshots at the processes that lasted centuries, it becomes clear that the fortunes of small peasants in these three countries varies over time and the condition of small peasants in the 19th century can no way be compared to that of the small peasants of today. Therefore, even though small peasants have always existed, their condition in the early

20th century is different from that during the Green Revolution which again is different from that of the post-globalization period. As Byres incisively notes, how useful is it to label the economic structure of the peasant agriculture in contemporary India 'semi-feudal' given that world-wide there is near monopoly of industrial capitalism?

I choose three historical instances to illustrate strikingly different experiences and paths of agrarian transformation and transition to capitalism. England, the first historical example of such transformation is seen as 'capitalism triumphant'–as landlord-mediated capitalism from below; Prussia, as the example of Lenin's celebrated 'capitalism from above'–and France as, 'capitalism delayed'. In general, Byres notes, conflict, rather than harmony, was the principal underlying feature of the relationship between the main classes of feudal society in Europe. Agrarian revolt was as natural to the seigneurial regime as strikes are to large-scale capitalism. In making this point, Byres runs against the fairly widespread current of academic thinking that sees feudal relations as peaceful, non-antagonistic and based on settled systems of obligation and patronage.

England: Landlord-Mediated Capitalism from Below

In the 13th century, the lower stratum of rich peasants held more than 30 acres, while a select few worked more than 60. The rich peasants controlled the commons, declared local custom, and maintained order through running the manorial court with its jurisdictional, punitive and land-registration functions. The existence of a sizeable market for agricultural products motivated them to accumulate more land, which they did through 'the abandoned demesnes (land usually around the manor) of the aristocracy', although, within the village community, there were limits upon the accumulation of land.

These new landlords expanded and reorganized their demesnes and employed professional agents who supervised them and ensured that the labour requirements of the lords was met through 'legally sanctioned coercive powers' to keep the flow of profits steady. Such increased demands, in turn, created discontent among the peasantry who also had other sources of social tension.

The earliest signs of resistance manifested in villeins–feudal tenants–raising disputes in royal courts about increased services demanded of them. Groups of such tenants argued that the lords could not make increased demands on them as under the law they also had rights. Therefore they argued that they were no ordinary villeins and so could not be subjected to the lord's arbitrary will. There was also resistance over the collection of Tallage[2], the right to buy and sell land, payment of merchet,[3] the attempt to extract labour rents fully; while there was collective refusal to perform services. Peasants kept breaking into manor houses and carry away charters, threatened to burn houses and harm the occupants physically. There were many instances of assault, and of 'violent defiance of both private and public authority'. Then, at the end of the 1340s, these social conflicts were intensified dramatically, by the savage impact of the Black Death, which cut the population by as much as 50 per cent. It induced additional seigniorial reaction to control tenants and labour thereby generating further class struggle between lords and peasants, partly giving rise to the English Rising of 1381. But, the 1381 rebels were defeated, and did not secure their goals.

These class struggles had their effect on rents, wages and the viability of feudal estates. Rents fell more or less universally between the early 14th and the early 16th century, making renting out of manorial land decreasingly profitable. Wages, too, rose over the long term. Even though agricultural prices had fallen by 10 per cent, real wages had multiplied by nearly two and a half times and cash wages had nearly doubled. For landlords whose demesne cultivation was increasingly done by wage labour, such 'rising wage cost' was of great significance. Landlords increasingly let out their demesne land for money rent, often on short leases, at competitive rents. Hilton refers to this as the 'collapsed seigniorial economy' of the 15th century. Many of the nobility went bankrupt. By the middle of the 15th century, there was a crisis, at least partly the result of a successful class struggle waged by the peasantry. Feudalism was no longer workable but the landlord class still owned preponderance of land. But what would take its place?

In a successful bid to make a turnaround in their falling rental income, the English landlord class transformed themselves from a feudal into a capitalist landlord class. By creating a competitive tenancy market, landlords dispossessed small and customary tenants of their rented land; instead letting it out in large units at higher rents on 'economic' leases. Such land, in order to be made suitable for capitalist farming, whether arable or pasture, was enclosed, either by the landlord himself, or by the new capitalist tenant, usually the latter. The entrapped small peasants bitterly resisted this enclosure. However, over time such struggles, be they against high rents, to facilitate seizing of land for pasture, or against enclosure, weakened. By the end of the Tudor era the transition had been completed, the new class structure was in place, and the way was set for the stark opposition, in the countryside, of the agricultural proletariat with the capitalist employer who was in alliance with a powerful capitalist landlord class. This is how the English agriculture transitioned to capitalism via a reconstituted landlord and capitalist tenant farmers classes.

In England, a feudal landlord class, rendered obsolete by class struggle waged by a united peasantry, was transformed into a progressive, capitalist landlord class. This class let its land, which was enclosed, in leases at 'competitive' rents. A rich peasantry (or, at least, its upper stratum), emerging from prior feudal differentiation, was metamorphosed into a class of capitalist tenant farmers able to pay 'competitive' rents and earn the average rate of profit. Integral to that outcome was the victory of the reconstituted landlord class over the peasantry during the 16th century, the era of transition.

France: Capitalism Delayed

The French countryside remained feudal until the late 19th century with small peasants (called manouvriers, who were owners of small holdings and hired themselves out as labourers) and middle peasants who owned horses and ploughs. Above them were differing categories of rich peasants with a tiny group of very rich peasants at 'the very peak of the peasant social pyramid'. These were a small class of large and enterprising tenants (operating 80-150 acres) in areas of large-scale farming: either the *laboureurs-fermiers* or the substantial tenant-farmers; the *receveurs de seigneurie* (the receivers for the lords of the manors), or *fermiers-receveurs* (farmer receivers). In the 18th century, the indebtedness of small peasants to larger ones increased. Increasingly small peasants hired themselves out as wage-labourers and there emerged a growing category of landless day-labourers, who worked for wages. In France, however, by 1789, the transition to capitalism did not occur.

Unlike in England, priests, nobles, and the bourgeoisie in France almost never managed their properties directly; their domains were extremely fragmented and rented-out as middle-sized farms, even as individual fields. Due to the absence of enclosures a very large number of small peasant proprietors survived. Between the French landlord class and the small peasantry was a class of middlemen called fermiers-généraux[4], comprising businessmen, notaries and shopkeepers. They stood between proprietor and sharecropper: leasing in sharecropping units from one or perhaps more than one proprietor and sub-letting them; perhaps assigned by the proprietor (if the proprietor was a lord) to collect seigneurial revenues; and entrusted with feudal rights of usage. The fermier-général, instead of encouraging commercial production, had a vested interest in the maintenance of the old system which guaranteed his own position.

The potential revolutionary role of tenant farmers in France was limited. Though squeezed by high rents, they remained attached to older feudal practices. It is the *laboureurs*, who owned horses and ploughs and made surplus who struggled for a change. They protested against the rack renting. There was a powerful movement for village enfranchisement with demands like fixation of judicial fines, abolition or regularization of the seigneurial tax, eradication of death duty, a fixed rather than arbitrary marriage tax, fixed payments to the lord on alienation of property. The demands also included 'freedom of personal status'.

The French Revolution cleared the ground for a possible unleashing of capitalism. It removed the massive barrier inherent in the feudal relationships which had persisted despite an apparently 'free' peasantry ('free' inasmuch as they were not serfs). It 'destroyed the seigneurial regime and abolished feudal rights, established the total right to property. It modified the distribution of land and proprietary rights in land, as church land and the land of émigré nobles were sold. The major beneficiaries were the urban middle class and the rich peasantry. Indeed, 'the French rural community' was destroyed. On the one hand, 'the *laboureurs* ... finally constituted themselves [as] a class', and clearly became the 'dominant class in the countryside'. On the other, "the 'mass of peasants'–a poor and middle peasantry–clung desperately to the traditional forms of production and stubbornly called for the maintenance of the limitations which collective constraints imposed on private property."

In France, a clearly unprogressive landlord class displayed no evidence of either transformation into a capitalist landlord class or a class of capitalist farmers; while the rich peasantry, a potential class of capitalists, was constrained, in part, by its surplus being effectively appropriated by the state and by landlords. This continued till 1789, while capitalist transformation was further postponed, till the end of the 19th century, by a relentless struggle waged by poor and middle peasants.

Prussia: Capitalism from Above

During the 11th-12th centuries, lay and church magnates obtained land grants in the east of Elbe, encouraged peasants in Rhineland and Low Countries to settle down there as free peasants. Known as Junkers, these 'colonizing German and Polish landowners created villages where the inhabitants were offered freer terms and conditions of life than in the western ones. Peasants were offered land holdings on free and heritable terms, on low money rents and their labour services and payments to church were waived. Superior jurisdictions and fiscal pressures were avoided. Instead of the landlord, his agent (who was given a holding three or four times the size of the peasants), became in effect the immediate lord, presiding over the village court and taking a proportion of the fines. (1973, 92).

The situation changed drastically in the 14th century in wake of the Black Death and other such visitations. There was widespread flight from land, leading to depopulated, deserted villages and a serious shortage of labour through the 15th century. The Junkers, leading the seigneurial offensive, began to acquire and farm deserted peasant land as an emergency measure till new peasants were found. However, when the corn prices began to rise in the 16th century it became more permanent. Confronted with a serious labour shortage, both of free wage labourers and of those employed via labour services, the Junkers curtailed peasants' freedom to move, imposed a wage limit, shifted from fixed money rents to competitive rents and, finally extended mandatory labour services of the peasants. By the 16th century, the wage labour multiplied and became the norm. The free peasantry disappeared completely.

However, the Prussian peasantry did not accept the deterioration of their rights and conditions without resistance. Appeals to princely/judicial authority had little effect and political uprisings were brutally suppressed. In this class struggle, the Junkers won a crushing victory. By the end of the 16th century, the Prussian Junkers had succeeded, with the aid of state power, in enserfing the free peasantry. The Junker economy developed as a form of seigneurial (feudal) market production in which, by means of extra-economic coercion, the landlords forced the peasantry to shoulder the cost of the labour, horsepower and tools necessary to demesne farming. When serfdom had broken down irretrievably in England and France, in Prussia it was re-established with a vengeance.

But, soon, a thin differentiation began to take place. A tiny minority of free peasants grew who frequently served the Junkers' interests as chief administrative and police officers and directing the village's labour. The unfree peasantry, divided into 'true Bauern', (the middle and large peasants owning 50-170 acres) and those who were not (holding 5-25 acres), i.e. the large class of marginal peasantry beneath the Bauern. All Bauerns had the obligation to maintain draught animals for the Junkers, a specified number according to the farm size.

Full and half Bauerns led the class struggle of peasants for the abolition of feudal obligations that began to threaten the feudal order by the second half of the 18th century. By the end of the 18th century the Prussian leadership realized that abolition of feudal dues was imperative. In 1807, in the wake of the crushing defeat by Napoleon's armies in 1806, feudalism was finally abolished—nearly 350 years after its demise in England, followed by a period of transition.

If the 16th century was the era of the transition to capitalist agriculture in England, the 19th century was so for Prussia. But in Prussia it was the erstwhile feudal landlords who became capitalist farmers. It was 'capitalism from above'. Let us see how this occurred in detail.

Junkers, just as the English landlord class, retained ownership of their land, enclosed the land of both poor and rich peasants, in the teeth of opposition, the land they owned and common land. But by the late 18th century, the Prussian nobility had accumulated much debt and in the severe depression of the 1820s the market for grains virtually collapsed, paving the way for decisive changes. A large number of noble estates had to be sold to the commoners. The new estate owners equipped with fresh capital led the way in the transformation of Prussian agriculture. By the 1850s, the proportion of Junker estates owned by commoners had tripled or quadrupled. By 1856 it stood at 56 per cent. But it was not only the new owners who took to capitalist farming. The old were similarly receptive to new ways.

The Prussian landlord class retained ownership of most of the land, engrossing large quantities of peasant land. But, unlike English landlords, they were takers of labour rent, i.e. they took decisions with respect to the form that production would take such as which crops would be grown, etc. Therefore, before 1807 they were not totally divorced from the process of production. Such a landlord class is more likely to transition to hiring wage labour than is the one with appropriates surplus via kind or money rent, which was prevalent in England. Such increase in rent seeking in cash led to the severing of links with production. They could also transition into a class of capitalist farmers but such a transformation is more likely where the landlord class has a direct relationship with labour (through labour rent) and has links with the process of production.

With the disappearance of obligatory labour services, Prussian landlords had lost their captive labour supply. Former serfs, indeed, were unwilling to work on Junker holdings. The relationship with the new forms of labour, however, was not immediately fully capitalist. It involved, initially and for some time, transitional forms. The Junkers, then, did not spring fully-caparisoned as capitalist farmers from the belly of feudalism. They would take time to slough off their feudal skins. At first, 'peasant labour services and the compulsory farm service of peasant youth on Junker farms were replaced by contractually hired farm servants and the cottager system...the latter [involving] the exchange of labour for an allocation of the land' (Perkins 1984, 5). While farm servants were technically free, there were restrictions on their movement.

This was followed by the system of confined labourers, hired on written short-term contracts. In each case, there was an absence of the money wage. Living standards were pitifully low. Ultimately, the Junkers were forced to employ day labourers, or 'free labourers' (frei Arbeiter), paid a money wage. It was wage labour, free in Marx's double sense, but not without the vestigial traces of feudalism. By 1871 the transition was complete. By then the Junkers were, in every useful sense, fully capitalist. It was a capitalism marked deeply by Prussia's immediate feudal past and the powerful subjugation of the peasantry which it entailed.

There were regions like in east of Elbe in Prussia, where free peasantry were initially brought by early colonizers, only to be enserfed later in the 16th century. Peasantry resisted the feudal exactions in the 18th-19th century, weakening Junkers. In response to eventual non-availability of serf labour, by the mid-19th century, the Junker class transformed itself into a class of capitalist farmers, farming with hired labour. The possibility of capitalism from below, via a rich peasantry, was wholly pre-empted by the absence of a rich peasantry of sufficient strength. The Junkers' first victory over the 'free' peasantry in the 16th century was marked by imposing feudalism, the 19th century victory over the enserfed peasantry was marked by the entry of capitalism–'capitalism from above'.

Conclusion

In England, a feudal landlord class, rendered obsolete by class struggle waged by a united peasantry, was transformed into a progressive, capitalist landlord class, which let its land, which was enclosed, in leases at 'competitive' rents; and a rich peasantry, emerging from prior feudal differentiation, was metamorphosed into a class of capitalist tenant farmers able to pay 'competitive' rents and earn the average rate of profit. Integral to that outcome was the victory of the reconstituted landlord class over the peasantry during the 16th century, the era of transition. In France, a clearly unprogressive landlord class displayed no evidence of either transformation into a capitalist landlord class or a class of capitalist farmers; while the rich peasantry, the *laboureurs*, a potential class of capitalists, was constrained, in part, by its surplus being effectively appropriated by the state and by landlords. This continued till 1789, while capitalist transformation was further postponed, till the end of the 19th century, by a relentless struggle waged by poor and middle peasants. In Prussia, a powerful feudal landlord class, the Junkers, having crushed, in the 16th century, the free peasantry that had existed east of the Elbe, and enserfed it comprehensively, eventually, in the 19th century, was transformed into a class of capitalist farmers; while the possibility of capitalism from below, via a rich peasantry, was wholly pre-empted by the absence of a rich peasantry of sufficient strength. The Junkers' decisive victory over the 'free' peasantry in the 16th century, which ushered in Prussian feudalism, was repeated in the 19th century over the formerly enserfed peasantry, in an equally crushing conquest, which was the prelude to a capitalism from above.

I have elsewhere sought to consider something of the relevance of the historical experience for contemporary developing countries (Byres 2002). I do not wish to repeat that here or seek to draw any detailed conclusions. Clearly, however, one must proceed with the utmost caution.

I can do no better, perhaps, than quote the late Rodney Hilton, the outstanding Marxist historian of feudal England, who had a formidable knowledge, too, of medieval Europe, and a keen interest in the contemporary world: "...Historians and sociologists are engaged in comparative studies of peasant societies in different epochs. It would be very risky to transfer any generalizations about peasant societies of medieval Europe to any other time. For example, the capitalist farmers who were to be an important element in the history of early European capitalism emerged in a general environment of small-scale enterprise. What could the fate of peasant societies in the present world of almost world-wide commercial and industrial monopoly capitalism have in common with that of peasant societies of the late medieval world? Clearly, the tasks of leadership in contemporary peasant society have nothing in common with the tasks of the past, except in the recognition that conflict is part of existence and that nothing is gained without struggle (1973, 236)".

To that I might add that when dealing with peasantries, in the past or the present, and however different the one is from the other, it is always important to consider the nature, the extent and the progress of the social differentiation that characterizes such peasantries, and the nature of the landlord class.

NOTES

1. Summarized from Terence Byres paper presented at the 2006 Workshop on 'The Peasantry and the Development of Capitalism in Comparative Perspective', as part of the International Conference on "Land, Poverty, Social Justice and Development", at the Institute of Social Studies, Hague. It is also published in *Journal of Peasant Studies,* Vol. 36, No. 1, January, 2009, pp. 33-54.
2. Tallage: A tax levied by the Norman and early Angevin kings of England on their Crown lands and royal towns.
3. A fine paid by a tenant in feudal England, especially a villein, to his lord for allowing the marriage of his daughter.
4. An outsourced tax collector in feudal France.

REFERENCES

Byres, Terence J., 2009. 'The Landlord Class, Peasant Differentiation, Class Struggle and the Transition to Capitalism: England, France and Prussia Compared', *Journal of Peasant Studies*, on 'Critical Perspectives in Agrarian Change and Peasant Studies', edited by Saturnino M. Borras Jr., Vol. 36, No. 1, January, 2009, 33-54.

Perkins, J.A., 1984. 'The German Agricultural Worker, 1815-1914', *Journal of Peasant Studies*, April, 11 (3): 3-27.

Byres, Terence J., 2002. 'Paths of Capitalist Agrarian Transition in the Past and in the Contemporary World', in V.K. Ramachandran and Madhura Swaminathan (eds.), *Agrarian Studies. Essays on Agrarian Relations in Less-Developed Countries*, 54-83, New Delhi: Tulika Books.

Hilton, Rodney, 1973. *Bond Men Made Free. Medieval Peasant Movements and the English Rising of 1381,* London: Temple Smith.

9

Agrarian Question: 'Then' and 'Now'

[Henry Bernstein]

> "[A]s the social formation comes to be dominated by industry and by the urban bourgeoisie, there ceases to be an agrarian question with any serious implications" [Byres, 1991:12]

> "[T]he agrarian question is an issue pertaining to capitalism and primarily to a period of transition or 'articulation' between capitalism and pre-capitalist modes of production" [Levin and Neocosmos, 1989:243]

The issue of the agrarian question poses a considerable intellectual challenge, both for understanding the diverse cases of agrarian transitions that happened historically, and for the ensuing transitions in contemporary poor countries. T.J. Byres has provided an important analytical framework, carefully teased out through close scrutiny of empirical and analytical differences in the six different paths of successful cases of transition in his book *Capitalism from Above and Capitalism from Below: An Essay in Comparative Political Economy* (1996) and also in his long engagement in the transition debate in the annals of *Journal of Peasant Studies*, as its editor. This essay, besides paying its tribute to his contribution, engages in unpacking multiple meanings of agrarian transition, builds to take discussion further over to the diverse contemporary predicaments; it seeks to complement the analytical discussion which is begun by Byres.

The Problematic

> [The] prospects in contemporary poor countries, are often considered of a limited number of 'paths' of capitalist agrarian transition: a set of paths already been traversed successfully in the past. The apparently essential features of these historically traversed paths are identified and are made to constitute the elements of models of possible agrarian transition...It has gradually seemed to me that the practice in this respect is defective, and misleading in two important ways. The first is that the paths in question–the 'models' of being taken to contemporary reality–are too few.....Not only that, but, secondly, the conception of these paths is too stereotyped and too narrow [Byres: 1996: pp. 3-4].

Byres has long been concerned with the agrarian question in the development of capitalism and with the economic development of the poor countries and committed to investigate both areas of study with analytical tools and methods of Marxist political economy. His contributions to these questions are, indeed, spread across his works, from historical debates, critical analysis of diverse cases across regions and time. Byres' problematic of the agrarian question, from his work, can be understood in three distinct meanings.

First, the early attempts, by the end of the 19th century, by European Marxists like Engels was to investigate the agrarian question from a political concern they were engaging with, how to accommodate the peasants in a working class led alliance for capturing political power. Engels already made a shift from the English model, which Marx analysed, in two respects. First, when it comes to France and Germany, where industrialization was not consequent on agrarian capital and wage labour that evolved through the capitalist transition in the agriculture, as was in the English case. The second modification was that, peasantries in mainland Europe were subject to new contradictions in their struggle for existence wrought by capitalist development and that resulted in (?) political alliances between workers and peasants, a move beyond the 'apathy of French small peasantry' mentioned by Marx in *The Eighteenth Bromaire* [Byres 1991].

The second meaning Byres derives is from the two historical texts, Kautsky's *The Agrarian Question* (1899) and Lenin's *The Development of Capitalism in Russia* (1964). The key concerns of Kautsky were the varied forms and effects of capitalist development in agriculture under capitalism; and the primary differences between capitalism in agriculture and industry. Lenin was concerned to demonstrate that 'capitalism could and actually was developing in Russia; his study was a part of polemics with *narodniks*, whose agrarian populism was confronted directly by Lenin's argument of capitalist class differentiation of the Russian peasantry.

Byres derives his third formulation from the scissors debate in the Soviet Union, from the work of Preobrazensky, who identified that the chief source of primary accumulation for the (socialist) industrialization lies outside the industry, which needs to be accomplished by transferring the net surplus from peasant agriculture through lower relative prices. This is supposed to facilitate a faster accumulation in industry. Byres was considerably inspired to investigate Preobrazensky's logic of industrial accumulation as an important part of the agrarian question. Even though, it was Kautsky and Lenin who were the first to study the capitalist development in agriculture, the absence of an understanding about the role of agriculture as the main source of primary accumulation for industry in their work is first noted by Byres.

This makes the radical core of Byres' reformulation of the agrarian question as: the role of agriculture in capitalist industrialization with and without 'the full development of capitalism in the countryside', in the sense of the dominance of social relations of production (agrarian capital and wage labour). Thus Byres goes on to suggest that "we can have a form of agrarian transition, a resolution in our third sense, such that the agrarian question appears to be resolved in neither the Engels nor the Kautsky-Lenin sense, but is resolved in this third sense in such a way that capitalist industrialization is permitted to proceed, then as the social formation dominated by industry and the urban bourgeoisie, there ceases to be an agrarian question with any serious implications. There is no longer an agrarian question in any substantive sense" [Byres, 1991; 12].

The purpose of this formulation is to escape the tyranny of the English path in which the capitalist order led to subsequent industrialization. Not only the possibility of the 'trinity' of capitalist landed property -tenant/-capitalist farmer/wage labour was exceptional, but the very logic of development of capitalism in agriculture as a precondition may be incapable of replication elsewhere and indeed unnecessary for industrialization in other circumstances.

Thus, the three meanings of the agrarian question that Byres raised can be delineated as the problematics of politics (AQ1), referring to building the necessary alliance between workers and peasants; (AQ2) referring to development of capitalist relations in agriculture; and (AQ3) contribution of agriculture to the industrial development. AQ2 includes all those issues related to development of productive forces in agriculture, such as technological innovation, production of marketable surplus, subsistence issues, working capital, development of markets, etc. For the primary accumulation (AQ3) it is not just what rate or mass of growth of agriculture commodities exchanged, but also their exchange price with manufacturing commodities–intersectoral terms of trade. This was precisely the debate raised by Preobrazensky in the Soviet context where he insisted pricing agriculture goods lower than manufacture to allow a faster accumulation in the latter. Agricultural growth stimulates the industrial growth by providing the demand for its goods, a process which was stressed by Lenin in his essay on formation of the home market for large-scale industry. We shall use this framework, to see the analytical differences in different paths in the following, which is presented in three sections.

Histories I

The challenge of this problematic of accumulation, given the substantial diversity, is pursued in a comparative overview of seven historical experiences of the successful agrarian transitions, namely, the English, French, Prussian, Japanese, Russian, American, South Korean and Taiwanese paths. The key themes analysed by Byres are:

i) nature of agrarian class structure and struggle prior to, during, and after transition; ii) characteristic forms of production during transition; iii) their effects on investment and productive forces; iv) how they are related to industrialization.

The English path followed the transformation of feudal into capitalist landed property with a distinctive feature that agrarian capital formed through differentiation of peasantry than from the landed property. This generated the class 'trinity' (landlord-capitalist tenant-wage labour) in which profits are generated by the capitalist tenant aided by the accompanying (progressive) landlord class. Exceptionally, a successful transformation of agriculture (in terms of AQ2) had preceded and contributed to the industrial accumulation (AQ3) in a long haul of almost two centuries.

The French path of feudalism was different, the peasant resistance to seigniorial offensive of the medieval period did not lead to any capitalist relations, as happened in England, instead resulted in consolidation of a sterile *rentier* landlordism. The French Revolution gave the small peasants a break from the feudal exactions, even if it did not lead to much differentiation among the small peasantry, but allowed them to persist through turbulence of market conditions beyond the 19th century's industrialization. The contribution of the agrarian sector to French industrialization remained insignificant, a matter that raises a question: how necessary is agrarian transition for the development of the industry?

The Japanese path was distinct in the pivotal role played by the state, during the Meiji Restoration of 1868, by taking a number of crucial steps necessary for a rapid industrial development, which was to take place subsequently. The state mediated the conflicts between the landlords and the tenants, invested in improving agriculture, prevailed over landlords to extract the surplus through taxes to be invested for the industrialization. Both the state and landlords had invested in agriculture and industry, productive forces were developed towards labour-intensive crops, that generated employment and export surplus. Byres notes the positive role played by the landlords, plausibly by the insistence of a forward-looking state, determined replicate a European style industrial development from the mid-19th century.

The Taiwan/South Korean paths originated in the land reforms implemented in the post-Second World War period under the Marshall Plan by the US. Even though, there was popular pressure to implement land reforms coming from the socialist counterparts, namely, the mainland China and North Korea; land reforms were seen as the means to unburden the peasant from rent but the peasants were subjected to ruthless state taxation and directed to primary accumulation for industrialization.

As one can see, all these instances of agrarian transition as paths out of feudal social relations exhibit considerable diversity. The exceptionalism of the English path and the unspecified contribution of the French path to industrialization cast as spotlight as East Asian experiences, which indeed approximate this extractive logic in Preobrazensky's model of primary accumulation on the back of the peasantry. In the case of Japan, landlords and the state through feudal intensification did the task of transferring the surplus, while in the case of Taiwan/South Korea land reforms removed the landlords and the surplus is extracted by the state to be transferred to industry.

Histories II

Byres, in his book, considered the Prussian and the American paths as two special cases, as they were proposed by Lenin to represent these two paths of capitalist transformation of agriculture (beyond English paths): a reactionary landlord path driven by the 'internal metamorphosis' of feudal class; and a 'peasant' (revolutionary) path that generated agrarian capital and labour through social differentiation.

The Prussian Junkers first encouraged 'free peasantry' to immigrate to bring the virgin lands in east of Elbe throughout the 15th-16th centuries, and began enserfing them by various ways towards the 17th century. Even as industrial transformation was happening in the other parts of Europe, which in turn was increasing commercial agriculture, it paradoxically intensified serfdom in these parts of Prussia towards the 18th century. Eventually, the defeat of Prussia in the hands of Napoleon's army and subsequent abolition of serfdom, compelled Junkers to shift to new methods of production. With increasing moral hazards and shirking from tenants, and the increased tax demand from the state, when Prussian wheat could not compete with English wheat. Thus the contradictions of insipid feudal extraction were intensified. All along the Junkers prevented any form of differentiation, by resisting any reform, and prevailed over the state to give a favourable terms of trade, forcing a reverse flow of surplus to agriculture. The pauperization of small peasantry under Junker domination led to stagnation of Department I and Department II (capital and consumer goods sectors, respectively) in German industry; on the whole this blunted the contribution of agriculture to industrialization. Lenin, called this as the reactionary path to capitalist transition. Interestingly, thus German industrial accumulation proceeded, not least because of agrarian transition, rather in spite of the perverse transition.

The American path represents another case, with a similarity and difference from the Prussian path. Even though the agrarian capital in the American path, in general, had formed through a process of primitive accumulation through dispossession of indigenous people, the initial attempts to secure feudal like labour (from the white immigrants) failed due to abundance of land. Then it had proceeded towards two regionally diverse paths. The southern states, which had dominance of plantation agriculture, did not see much industrial development right through the 19th century, as slavery removed incentives to either modernize agriculture or invest in the industrial capital, like in the Junker path. The planters lacked entrepreneurial interest to use free wage labour that would potentially threaten the facility of slave use. American plantation slavery is, therefore, another parallel to the 'second serfdom' of Prussia, both interestingly ending with military defeats.

The American Civil War and the subsequent abolition of slavery in 1865 eventually made the southern planters to shift to sharecropping; renting farms to erstwhile slaves. Yet, the planters continued to squeeze exorbitant surplus from tenant farmers through multiple means like, restricting the size of the holdings, denying off-farm employment, rack renting, changing tenants through yearly contracts, direct supervision of labour process and perpetuating debt bondage. These tenants, were finally financially crushed by the slump during the Great Depression of 1930. Byres refers to this as akin to 'interlinked modes of exploitation' stated by Amit Bhaduri and Krishna Bharadwaj in the Indian context. The reactionary character of the plantation owners in southern US continued to be reflected in slower adoption of mechanization, newer techniques and consequent lower productivity growth; all rooted in the nature of the labour process. This kind of sharecropping lasted till the 1940s.

Thus, in the southern US case, even after the Civil War, the accumulation regime was controlled by the same landowners who were hostile to economic development that competes for labour, by restricting the scope of development through immobilizing labour and interlocked tenancy markets. Only in the second half of the 20th century, did rapid mechanization finally displace sharecroppers with an expansion of cotton farming and formation of more dynamic agrarian capital. Like in the Prussian path, the formation of agrarian surplus appropriation in the American south, did not contribute much to industrialization.

In contrast, in the north and mid-west, petty commodity production underwent a transformation in the early 19th century, through rising land prices, taxes, cost of establishing new farms and increased commodification of farm services. The transition was powered by rapid development of productive forces and costs of labour. This remarkable expansion provided the vital stimulus to industrialization, both in terms of demand as well as supply of agro-industrial raw materials. Farm tools, machinery, floor mills, leather tanning, meat packing, canning, bailing machinery, etc., constituted almost a quarter of industrial demand by 1870. An important point to note is the fact that despite the considerable technical advancement and extremely competitive capitalist development, to everyone's surprise, the (small farm) petty commodity production did not disappear, but survived. Even while Lenin noted this distinguishing trend in his analysis, he could not anticipate the ability of petty commodity production to survive past the advancement in industry.

Byres makes an important departure from Lenin while making a comparative discourse between Prussian and American paths, by shifting the focus to the question of accumulation (AQ3) from transformation of agriculture (AQ2). Byres notes that in the Prussian case too, as with the American one, the stimulus for industrialization in the 1850s had not come from the Junkers in the east of Elbe, but from the petty commodity producers in western Prussia, and the territorial expansion during the German unification. Therefore, in both cases the intensification of petty commodity production, rather than the accumulation by Junkers or plantation owners, provided the stimulus to industrialization. Finally, the powerful contribution of American agriculture to its industrialization is actually provided through effective forward-backward linkages between agriculture and industry. This bestows an extraordinary 'virtuous' quality on the American path of agrarian transition and its forms of accumulation, where nothing so much of sequencing of agrarian transformation actually happened in Preobrazensky's logic for industrial accumulation, which Byres sees central to East Asian paths.

Histories III

What are the lessons from these historical experiences of agrarian transition for the contemporary poor countries? Byres cautions against choosing any of these paths to be models to be followed, despite the fact that agrarian transition has definite influence on the nature of the capitalist industrialization.

Byres argued that the English path is ruled out for India, at least in the areas where Permanent Settlements were implemented. The Junker path could be applicable to countries in Latin America, and ones like Pakistan in Asia (which failed to implement land reforms). At the same time, Byres argues that a successful peasant path could be a possibility for poor countries, if the state plays a progressive role against powerful social, political and economic interests of the landlord class, combined with a sustained class struggle by the peasants. There could be peasant capitalisms and differentiation, as in Lenin's (northern) US path (AQ2) and India as illustrated by the Green Revolution in north western India (AQ2), with a stubbornly resisting and surviving small peasant economy, as in France.

By conflating the agrarian sector's transformation (AQ2) with agriculture's contribution to industry (AQ3) in this way here, there could be some slippages. The paths defined as that of agrarian transition do not qualify as paths of transition in the strong sense, formulated as AQ3. Examples already given in the Prussian path (a reactionary variant of AQ2), and the slavery/sharecropping based plantation in the American south, indeed proved obstacles to capitalist development. Another example is that of the French path, where small peasants aspire to be a part of capitalist commodity relations and class differentiation. Their paths neither satisfies AQ2 nor AQ3. Therefore, Byres' own framework is underdetermined, in the sense, future history may present further possibilities.

The Analytics of 'Then' And 'Now'

Let's see the conditions of transformation in the past and that of the present. 'Then' and 'now' in the problematic of agrarian transaction starts with multiple possibilities in paths and sequences. There are three main clusters of questions related to AQ2 and AQ3 in Byres' framework, such as:

First:
- (i) Growth of agricultural production and productivity (AQ2)

Second:
- (ii) Terms of trade between agriculture and industry (AQ3)
- (iii) Development of demand for agricultural products (AQ3)
- (iv) Freeing of *agricultural labour* to join the urban proletariat (AQ3)

Third:
- (v) Surplus appropriation in agriculture (AQ2)
- (vi) Surplus *transfer from* agriculture to industrial accumulation (AQ3)

The range of substantive paths of agrarian transitions can be viewed in terms of different combinations of those moments in the order of their virtuosity. First, Preobrazensky's logic appears to be a limiting case: it centres on: (i) the surplus transfer from agriculture, (ii) the terms of trade and (iii) imposing levies and administered prices as the only critical instruments of primary accumulation for industry. Further, in terms of *sequencing*, the growth of productivity and the demand for industrial products have to await the prior development of industry.

Among the East Asian cases, the Japanese one is a little unusual and unique in the character of the landlord class, which was to *reinvest* their rental income in industry and in land augmentation. This is to be complemented by a crucial role in investing in rural infrastructure, help improve the productivity and the export surplus. The agrarian transition is completed before the industrial development began taking place. The role of the state continued to be crucial in transferring the surplus for industrialization development. The Japanese case reminds us again that the agrarian transition had no simultaneous role in complementing the industry.

The exceptionally virtuous quality of the American path was possible with strong 'backward-forward linkages' (based on balanced terms of trade, rather than an adverse terms of trade for family farms).

Further, there could be differences in speed of adjustment in transition such as the English path, landlords probably had the leisurely course of more than a century and a half period towards becoming 'progressive' landlords, while Junkers in the Prussian path were quickly swamped by the industrial development in the 19th century. Similar are the cases of Japan, South Korea and Taiwan, where agrarian transition took a much shorter duration. Therefore, even the diversity of these six cases goes beyond what Byres himself contemplates.

The analytical moments of Byres, in our discussion, make a few things very clear. The potential of agriculture to play a decisive role in overall capitalist development is not quite clear. There is nothing which in fact guarantees the surplus appropriation in agriculture to necessarily result in the transfer of its surplus to industry, as illustrated by the Junkers' path and southern plantation owners in the US. Absence of conditions that enabled the virtuous path of American (north), had blocked agrarian transition and industrialization in the south. Such obstacles are also the Indian case, illustrated by the inability of the Indian state to tax agriculture incomes, even while facing a severe resource constraint for the planned development after independence. Far from these stand points, one need not always expect agriculture alone to play the role of sheet anchor for industrial development, sometimes, in history the merchant capital played that role of primary accumulation for industry.

Besides the timing, sequencing and duration of agrarian transition, the complexity of factors, given the diversity they display in different cases, also requires a deep class analysis and in addition, a study of the role and nature of the state. Here lies the key question of figuring out the configuration of social forces that promote or hinder the agrarian transition. The agrarian transition that took place across time and space differs in terms of social formation that gives rise to differences in sequencing and outcomes. Further, development of capitalism at some places would influence the capitalist development elsewhere which also causes these differences. International/transnational comparisons should be complemented by the investigation and explanation beyond the internal dynamics. As in the Prussian case, the reactionary role of Junkers was also complemented by their key role of providing leadership in state formation and expansion. Plantation slavery could have blocked industrialization in the American south but had contributed to the industrialization in Britain and later on, to the American road to capitalism. As Perry Anderson suggested, both examples present a case of uneven and combined development in Europe; then the New Plantation slavery based on capitalist development on a world scale.

Uneven and Combined Development on a World Scale

It will be worthwhile to note the uneven and combined development on a world scale to see the role of many different starting points of capitalist development, central for the formulation of substantive diversity in Byres' comparative investigation. However, it needs to be complemented by location of the transition on a world scale and its timing and the issue of 'then' and 'now'.

In Byres' six cases of successful transitions, with the exception of South Korea and Taiwan, all the rest have completed their transition by end of the 19th century. They also encompassed multiple sources of primary accumulation from territorial expansion, international trade, colonial plunder and surplus extraction as well as from their own agrarian structures.

For the European ex-colonies of Asia and Africa, besides the different starting points of the incorporation in the surplus extraction and their moments of getting independence, where they stand in the course of development remain varied. For many of these turning to their national development plan after decolonization are also faced with several difficulties. They would lose the external sources for primary accumulation and be forced to face the technological advanced world markets. Any dependence on external sources for investment and technology would impinge on the nature and type of industrialization. The effects of intersectoral linkages between agriculture and industry would be mediated by the different effects of the circuits of international capital and world markets for each sector in any capitalist economy (in the entre or periphery of world capitalism).

In short, modern imperialism shapes the prospects of industrialization in contemporary poor countries, beyond agrarian transformation. The substantive diversity in forms of agrarian change and their contribution to the industrial accumulation by the relatively 'virtuous' or 'vicious' means (based on growth and intersectoral linkages) in the imperialist periphery also shapes their prospects. This is the predicament of contemporary poor countries located in Asia and Africa.

Many of them are yet to experience a comprehensive industrialization. Their migration and urbanization pattern stand in stark contrast with the demographic trajectories of historic agrarian transition. The kind of intensive production techniques adopted in developed countries geared to meet global markets, is yet to be seen in poorer regions of the world. Some of them could not even achieve a scale of self-sufficiency.

The colonial and imperialist systems had integrated several regions of the world and the process has indeed continued the job through the current times of globalization. In this context, Harriet Friedmann and McMichael's (1989) contribution is of great significance. They argued in their analysis that, historically, there are three vital global food regimes in the post-industrial revolution period. The first phase is that of 1870-1945, where the massive import of grain and livestock production were mobilized from the vast frontier settler states like Argentina, Australia and USA to Europe. Exports from these competed with temperate regions of the European homelands as well as with those from the colonies in Asia and Africa, whose incorporation into global food regimes was completed during the same period. This first food regime lasted till 1941, when it was subverted by European interests through the cheaper imports and disruptions of the First World War, and Great Depression of 1930. This disruption led to a flurry of measures of protection and regulation to help farmers to cope with fluctuations of global markets in several countries, in subsequent times.

The second international food regime began after 1945, which was characterized by the American grain exports to Latin America, newly independent Asia and Africa. The US leveraged its exports using Aid as the mechanism, to gain larger traction in establishing hegemony under Cold War conditions. This shift was partly a result of a continuing nationalist trajectory of strategic protectionism followed by Europe. This regime too came to an end with rising costs of production in the US, re-entry of EC into export markets and a degree of nationalist self-sufficiency achieved by a number of post-colonial countries, especially in Asia.

The third regime which extends to contemporary times, is a wheat based/wage goods regime integrated by transnational capital, involved in building and forming international food chains. The integration of agro-industrial food chains first occurred in advanced countries and later incorporated certain peripheral and post-socialist countries also into this. Thanks to the cheapening of transport technologies, even the perishable agrarian products are integrated into global food chains. Now the prospects of the peasantry are determined by this additional factor–the global market, besides the domestic.

Thus, this regime amplifies the uneven and combined development taking place on a world scale, breaching boundaries of national economies and also the cross-sectional boundaries of agriculture and industry. In this scenario, is there still an agrarian question at the end of the 20th century? Through its journey in times of international and global restructuring of agriculture appear to imply the death of the agrarian question, as informed by the histories recorded. One can reinforce this implication with a hypothesis that the agrarian question of capital is transcended by the generalized commodity relations on a global place–in the countryside of Africa, Asia as in that of the industrial countries.

An important point to be observed is the fact that the uneven and combined development on a global level presents some peculiar possibilities: that the prospect of industrial development is not contingent on agrarian transition–in short, end of the agrarian question, without its resolution.

End of the Agrarian Question?

Even as Lenin was writing on the Prussian and American paths, he was extremely aware about the contribution of the political class in forming the formal and informal institutions such as law, state policy, business culture, strategic and military leadership, and so on, the understanding that the AQ1 is articulated in such a manner that AQ2 and AQ3 as immanent to the political question. The Junker class, for instance, even as being a reactionary power regarding AQ2 and AQ3, played an extremely critical role in becoming a remarkably united class in building the military and political state of Germany [Anderson]. The socio-cultural and political contribution towards militarism, anti-Semitism, building a strong state between world wars conveys the complex role of the agrarian question of politics that addresses contradictions of other agrarian questions [Gerschenkron]. Likewise, in the American case, the politics of civil war could not resolve the 'unfreedom' of black labour, which reappeared in the form of share cropping. The New Dealers resolved to subsidize the agriculture in a big way in the post-war period, and resolve it entirely in a new way by encouraging modernization and provisioning a stable market in its Cold War/ Aid politics.

Similarly, for the case of poor countries, one need not be led towards any deterministic logic reflected in a 'World System' sense that places the periphery in a strait jacket of underdevelopment. National development policies in the post-colonial period have partially addressed the issues of AQ2 and AQ3. Taking these further ahead, the globalization and integration to global supply chains, is capable of producing effects to last beyond formal subsumption. The analysis of dynamics of global capital and its stage of modern imperialism, generates issues which must inform consideration of all three agrarian questions, without predetermining the outcome. First, one should look at how national economies articulate their interests, markets, international linkages, forms of accumulation and effectiveness of state–are all shaped by their location in the world economy. This will reveal the relative effects at the centre and the periphery of imperialism and within them.

Conclusion

By way of conclusion, a different juxtaposing of the three agrarian questions is suggested. Just as Byres demonstrates the possibility of agrarian transition with or without capitalist transformation of agriculture (AQ2), one can pose the salience of AQ1 and AQ2 with or without agrarian transition. The agrarian question or problematic is in effect the agrarian question of capital, especially industrial capital. The AQ3–the transformation of agriculture, as a source of accumulation for industrial capitalism–specifically of industrial capital, has now assumed predominance. It is, in fact, resolved on the global plane of contemporary imperialism. The agrarian question that Lenin posed is the agrarian question of working masses–proletarians and peasants, which is important for democracy, just as it was important to build the worker-peasant alliance to make industrialization built on the socialist primitive accumulation.

In the contemporary post-colonial periphery, capitalist development from above or the vicious class struggles in the countryside generated by peasant capitalism cannot provide the peasant an escape from poverty and misery. Such capitalist development may be backward, plagued by landlordism and the agrarian transition may not have been complete. Under any and all these conditions the conditions of the peasants will continue to be miserable as the current moment is characterized by generalized commodity production on a global level. Caught within the logic of the accumulation designed to extract surplus for the non-farm sector, the peasant will be waging a losing battle. The urgency of bread and democracy will continue to distinguish the agrarian questions of the working masses and to drive their struggles.

[This is a shortened essay by Henry Bernstein, titled 'The Agrarian Question: Then and Now', in Bernstein, Henry and Tom Brass edited *Agrarian Questions: Essays in Appreciation of T.J. Byres*, Frank Cass Publishers, London, 1996, pp. 22-59]

10

The Agrarian Question Under Globalization[1]

[Haroon Akram-Lodhi and Cristobel Kay]

Where Do We Begin?

More than a century ago, for Karl Kautsky the agrarian question meant 'whether and how capital is seizing hold of agriculture, revolutionizing it, making old forms of production and property untenable and creating the necessity for new ones' (Kautsky, 1889. See summary in this volume). A century later, for Terence J. Byres (1996. strike down), it was the 'continued existence of obstacles in rural areas in a substantive sense, (preventing) accumulation both within agriculture and outside in industry' that was the core of the agrarian question. In the age of globalization, does capital still transform the peasantry as national capital did at certain historical junctures, or do peasants continue to survive as petty commodity producers? AL and K argue that globalization produces a complex dynamic that integrates the peasantry within global markets, intensifying their crisis beyond relegating them to reserve an army of labour. For the authors, it is peasant resistance to the logic and imperative of their marginalization by capital that constitutes the core of the contemporary agrarian question.

The Peasant Question in Classical Marxism: Differentiation and Transformation

AL and K begin by charting the important trajectories of capitalism's entry into European societies, as theorized by Marx, Engels,

Kautsky and Lenin. This entry transformed the organization of agrarian production and the lives of peasants in different ways. Multiple political regimes and the imperialist expansion through colonization led to multiple trajectories of capitalist transition in agriculture. The authors contest the popular understanding that Marx viewed peasantry as 'a pre-capitalist remnant that will be dragged into modernity by the capitalist mode of production'. They direct our attention to the better and more fully developed view of Marx, which appeared in *Capital*, Vol. I:

> All revolutions are epoch making that act as levers for the capitalist class in course of formation. But this is also true for those moments when great masses of men are suddenly and forcibly separated from their means of subsistence and hurled into the labour market as free, unprotected and rightless proletarians. The expropriation of the agricultural producer or the peasant, from the soil is the basis of the whole process. The history of this expropriation assumes a different order of succession and at different historical epochs. Only in England which we therefore take our example, has it in the classic form [Marx 1976, 876].

AL and K also direct our attention to the observation of Marx that capital does not destroy peasant classes in some regions, but subsumes the labour of peasant classes using 'hybrid' modes of surplus extraction. Reading Marx's (1881) letters to his correspondent Vera Zasulich (https://www.marxists.org/archive/marx/works/1881/zasulich/) on the fate of the Russian peasantry in rapidly industrializing Russia enables us to see his deep insight into the possibilities of multiple resolutions of the agrarian question for small-scale peasant producters.

What is interesting and useful in Akram-Lodhi and Kay's method is their attention to the historical context of each theoretical formulation.

They note that Engels examined the agrarian question in the context of the internationalization of the food regime, resulting from European imperialist expansion, which began to undermine peasant livelihoods in Europe (See Engels in this volume for more details).

Kautsky (1880) and Lenin (1889), who arrived later in the century, focused on the continuing transformation of agriculture in the wake of industrial capitalism. They saw capitalist industrialization breaking the traditional link between agricultural and rural petty manufacturing by commodifying the former and linking it to distant markets (See Kautsky in this volume for more details). For them, industrial capitalism thus propelled agrarian capitalism.

Next, AL and K also delineate the distinct ways in which these classical thinkers identified the coping and surviving mechanisms of the peasantry under industrial capitalism. They note Marx's identification of social differentiation between households, which transform into accumulating households and those which fail and struggle to sustain their subsistence; Kautsky's identification of self-exploitation of the small peasantry and the intensification of rural production under industrial capitalism, where the agrarian question gets linked to imperialist world markets; and Lenin's identification of class differentiation in agriculture between exploiting big landlords and rich capitalist farmers and exploited classes of small tillers and landless labour. For both Kautsky and Lenin, they point out, agrarian capital need not rely on dispossessing petty commodity producing peasants.

The Peasant Question in Planned Economies: Socialist Primitive Accumulation

If industrial capitalism the world over made accumulation faster by repressing the relative prices of farm products, created through unfettered competition among peasants and the opening up of market for imports, what the countries that embarked on planned growth did is another question that AL and K explore. The obvious case for them is the Soviet Union.

AL and K note that a situation arose after the formation of the Soviet Union when the planners had to make a decision on the role of agriculture and the peasantry. Under the New Economic Policy peasants began to enjoy favourable prices from rising urban demand. Industrialization and shortages of agricultural goods led to a sharp rise in agricultural prices. Such an increase vis-a-vis manufactured goods prices slowed down accumulation in industry. Even as Bukharin argued against imposing any curbs on food prices, favouring a long-term balance of prices, Evegy Preobrazensky, a Marxist economist in Russia and a contemporary of Bukharin, argued that for the modern industrial sector to accumulate, agricultural prices had to be kept relatively low. The industrial sector was seen as a harbinger of development that would accommodate the surplus labour evicted from agriculture as relative prices moved against agriculture. Preobrazensky called this "socialist primitive accumulation". This advice was implemented through forced collectivization which involved violence, the incarceration of resisting farmers, and widespread death.

The Agrarian Question After Lenin: A Debate Among Historians

AL and K note that after Lenin it was primarily historians who debated capitalist transition. The focus was on two issues. The first was to understand what led to the fall of feudalism in Europe; and the second was to understand the rise of capitalism as a different form of surplus creation and appropriation. Maurice Dobb in 1963 argued that feudalism ended in England because of conflicting social relations between feudal lords and peasants: feudal exaction in the form of rents led to violent clashes with peasantry. Eventually, the small peasantry were expropriated from their holdings through land enclosures established by the landlords, and were reduced to wage labour, while a better off class of free peasants emerged as capitalist tenants to lease in the lands of lords. Rodney Hilton (1976) marshalled archival evidence for the conflict which is described as class struggle by Dobb. The class struggle led to a change in production relations to allow the productive forces to grow. However, Paul Sweezy (1976) contended that it was the emergence of long distance trade towards the middle of the 15th century that enabled change to happen, suggesting that external factors in the sphere of exchange played the key role.

In 1976, Robert Brenner reopened the debate after studying the European transition more comprehensively and produced a much more rounded explanation within historical materialism. Brenner identified the development of private property rights and class differentiation as crucial moments that brought a resolution to the conflict. Private property rights, granted by the state, created incentives to lords to make improvements to their lands and enter clear contractual relations with the free peasantry leasing their lands. Thus, it was the changes in class structure, and in class relations, that, in Brenner's view, brought a resolution to the class struggle of feudalism.

The Agrarian Question in the Late the 20th Century[2]

Noting that by the end of the 20th century, a new understanding of the agrarian question developed, extending the classical account, AL and K draw attention to the important analytical distinctions made by Bernstein in the agrarian question along the lines of three 'problematics', before moving on to outline what they think are the crucial agrarian problematics for the 21st century. Bernstein made these distinctions while reviewing the corpus of T.J. Byres' writings on multiple capitalist transitions in Europe, Asia and North America.

AQ1 *the problematic of 'accumulation'* (the 'agrarian question' is called AQ in general in this essay) is derived from Preobrazhensky's theory of socialist primitive accumulation. This analyses agriculture's potential ability to generate 'surplus output' and a 'financial surplus' over and above its own requirements. This supports industrialization, structural transformation, accumulation and the emergence of capital both within and beyond agriculture.

AQ2 *the problematic of 'production'* has its origin in Kautksy, Marx and Lenin's works. This analyses the extent of capitalist development in the countryside, the form that it takes and the barriers to its development. It looks at the micro political economy issues affecting the structural transformation of petty commodity producing peasant labour into its commodified form through rural labour processes [the large body of empirical work in the 'mode of production debate in India' falls into this category].

AQ3 *the problematic of 'politics'* is drawn from the theoretical works of Engels. The dynamics between structures of dominance, subordination and surplus appropriation and the agency of social classes in the transformation lie at the centre of this problem. So the political struggles against feudal oppression for resources which eventually contribute to agrarian transition constitute the question of politics [The classical debate about the balance of class forces, the debate between Dobb and Sweezy, and later Brenner's critique, falls under this question].

This increasing analytical clarity provided by Bernstein on the agrarian question, AL and K note, had made it possible to imagine multiple transformatory possibilities by the end of 1990s. One could have transformation, non-transformation, or the partial-transformation of petty commodity producers into wage labour. Hence, labour power was created through complex forces of dispossession. Once peasants or other rural petty commodity producers were unable to produce a sufficient fraction of their consumption needs, they had to start selling their labour power to buy basic needs (food or other needs) that they previously produced themselves. Such wage labour would be sold to an urban employer, a rural capitalist farmer, or rural non-farm enterprises. Thus, rural petty commodity producers (peasants, artisans, service providers) are transformed into wage labour or agrarian proto-capitalists. This happens under a market that works with its own logic and which becomes a necessary destination for their products and labour.

In short, it is the commodification of labour which underpins the deeper process of generalized commodity production as well as the concomitant transformation in the process of production–from production for use to production for exchange and accumulation. The agrarian transition is hence a process by which this does or does not occur, as well as its implications for accumulation and the emergence of capital. In this sense, AL and K argue, Bernstein (2004) framed the agrarian question of capital initially as the emergence of capital and later expanded it to the reproduction of capital, which is predicated on appropriation. It is also important to examine the way in which accumulation, production and politics contribute to or are constrain the agrarian transition.

The Agrarian Question Under Globalization

AL and K argue that globalization has transformed the development of the forces and relations of production on a world scale. How then has globalization changed the conditions for agrarian transition in the late 20th century?

In the heydays of Keynesianism during the 1950s and 1960s, land reforms and the distributional interventions of the state were seen in line with boosting the aggregate demand. By the 1980s, a home market-based state-led capitalist development strategy was replaced with export-led market-led strategies of production. By encouraging agricultural exports in Africa, Asia and Latin America through varieties of policy-conditionality based on loans, international agencies like the IMF and World Bank have managed a reintegration of agricultural production with global markets. By facilitating international repayment mechanisms, giving access to investments and promoting technical change, new strategies have managed to enhance productivity, production and profits [World Bank 2007, Akram-Lodhi 2008, Veltmeyer 2009].

In this context, AL and K find it imperative to ask, as with Bernstein (1996), whether, under neoliberal globalization, agrarian transition is possible or even relevant for contemporary poor countries?

The first key issue is that over the second half of the 20th century, agriculture was effectively 'decoupled' from the problem of capital accumulation. The authors note that capital accumulation in the periphery is today driven by manufacturing and services on a world scale. Capital, now globalized and connected with transnational capital, does not require access to surplus agricultural resources in order to facilitate accumulation. It therefore no longer needs to reorganize agricultural production. Agrarian transition is no longer the necessary pre-condition for development of capitalism. Rather, transnational capital requires the technical capacity to ever more efficiently allocate resources on a global scale to enhance the mass and rate of surplus value and its realization (Araghi 2009).

The second key issue is implicitly embedded in the first. The internationalization of capital has 'decoupled' transnational capital from national labour regimes, which are becoming ever more fragmented. They become helpless in providing a livelihood. It is not that agriculture does not matter for global capital accumulation; but by segmenting labour on a global scale, enlarging the global reserve army and fostering a crisis of reproduction among the fragmented classes, it can appear that transnational capital has made the agrarian question redundant in the old sense. Agrarian question needs to be reconfigured for the contemporary conditions.

In this context, AL and K identify seven different and competing analytical approaches that are being followed and used by theorists to frame the contemporary agrarian question.

Seven Agrarian Questions in Globalization?

AQ1: *The Agrarian Question of Class Forces*

It is argued here that the articulation of forces and relations of production can take place in complex and multifaceted ways. Transition is contingent and subject to diversity even on a global level. By implication, it becomes necessary to understand the diverse and uneven ways in which rural production processes are transforming (or not) into the capitalist mode of production. These processes must be globally contextualized. Social differentiation, the nature of the landlord class, market imperatives and the severity of law of value, and the character of the state all matter in the framework of this mode of formulating the agrarian question.

In short, AQ1 investigates ongoing peasant differentiation and the emergence of rural capitalism,

AQ2: *The Path-Dependent Agrarian Question*

Articulated by Bill Warren this approach argues that imperialism through colonialism introduced capitalist relations of production throughout the world. Even though this process was uneven across time and space, it has unleashed an inexorable, if contingent and dynamic, process of labour commodification across developing countries. Thus the ongoing expansion of wage labour signals that the capitalist mode of production is deepening in rural worlds and transforming agrarian production systems. No part has been left untransformed.

AQ2 focuses on the struggle to resist de-peasantization and later that of wage labour under rural capitalism.

AQ3: The Global Reserve Army of Labour Agrarian Question

Farshad Araghi (2009) initiated this question by arguing that the unchallenged neoliberal globalization of today is the direct continuation of liberal imperialism witnessed in the 19th century. So the periods 1834 to 1870 and 1973 to the present have the following in common: economic liberalism, anti-welfarism, free-market fetishism, and a global division of labour through 'workshops of the world'. Araghi argues that the modern forms of neoliberal globalization have constructed an 'enclosure food regime' that produces, transfers and distributes value on a world scale. The enclosure food regime has established subsidized consumption and overconsumption among the classes of the global North. This also created global 'slums' and an global unemployed reserve army, who migrate globally for their livelihood. Thus the agrarian question is reproduced under more demanding terms.

AQ3 adopts a capital-centric perspective over protracted struggles to dispossess small producers from the realm of farm production.

AQ4: The Decoupled' Agrarian Question of Labour

This question, raised by Bernstein, argues that under the globalized capitalist regime that reintegrates national capital with transnational capital, the capitalist transformation of agriculture has become irrelevant and redundant for broader capitalist transformation in the developing countries. Agrarian capital is a subordinated entity and has limited influence on the alignment of class forces in the countryside, even though it influences and changes production relations. Thus, Bernstein prioritizes a 'rural politics problematic' over a 'production and accumulation problematic'.

AQ4 sees a struggle between globalizing capitalism and peasants pauperized within global value chains.

AQ5: *The Corporate Food Regime Agrarian Question*

This is associated with Phillip McMichael (2009). Like Araghi, McMichael argues that the agrarian question should be reconfigured within the global context. Unlike Araghi, McMichael stresses the specific historical condition of financialization, neoliberalization and the creation of a 'global food regime' that fosters a commodity accumulation 'fetish' in agriculture. Corporate food regimes operate in an enclosed space of high-end markets, excluding the poorer masses. Global capital movements organize these corporate food regimes. The peasant economy is reproduced by the terms dictated by the corporate food regime.

AQ5 also uses a world historic perspective on the agrarian question of food as a struggle over rural livelihoods and globalizing generalized commodity production of labour and capital.

AQ6: *The Agrarian Question of Gender*

This is a variation of the earlier problematic raised by Bridget O'Laughlin (2009), who argued that the accumulation, production and politics have considerable gender dimensions. The non-commodified unpaid labour of women for families makes a considerable contribution to the creation of value. The politics of the agrarian question should at least understand and raise the issue of gendered division of labour.

AQ6 is critical of the conception of prevaling notions of struggle, bringing in a gender dimension.

AQ7: *The Agrarian Question of Ecology and Environment*

The agrarian production, accumulation and rural politic problematics have another dimension, namely the biophysical agro-ecological setting, which influences the assets, production process and class formation. The myopic commercial regime that uses up agro-ecological resources through unsustainable technologies will begin posing limits on the rate of accumulation. The agrarian question must address, in light of the ecological degradation caused by corporate agricultural practices, the character of ecological relationships and contradictions of class and ecology. (Pearse 1985, Tony Weis 2007 and Bellamy Foster 2009)

AQ7 suggests that the political ecology of struggle is shaped by biophysical contradictions in capitalism that are integral to understanding the agrarian question.

To arrive at the the contemporary relevance of the agrarian question, AL and K argue, one has to assess the complementarities and conflicts embedded between and among the seven agrarian questions, all of which are capable of offering insights into transformation.

The Agrarian Question in the 21st Century

AL and K argue that neoliberal globalization and the global agricultural export regimes that are produced have led to more capital-intensive production. It has increased peasant differentiation, pulling some petty commodity producers into global supply chains, while getting many entangled in a viability crisis of indebtedness, poverty and semi-proletarianization. This has occurred throughout the developing countries as export markets have replaced home markets.

Tropical products like cocoa, tea, coffee, spices, maize, and sugar, and temperate products like milk, cheese, edible oils, animal feeds, fish, sea foods, fruits and vegetables, tobacco and cotton, are all linked to global supply chains. Global agro-business corporations coordinate the supply chain management through extending backend infrastructure, cold chains, and contract farming. All this reorientation is aiding rural accumulation among capitalist farms as well as distress among the petty commodity producers. When capital restructures globally, the mobilization of the agricultural surplus is also being globalized.

AL and K further argue that despite the ongoing systemic global subsistence crisis of the 21st century, there is not going to be the 'death of peasantry,' as historian Eric Hobsbawm predicted. There are other trends at work: decollectivization and repeasantization in post-socialist countries like Vietnam, and Central Asia, on the one hand; and semi-proletarianization and fragmentation without full polarization on the other. All these represent a reconfiguration of livelihoods, deepening market imperatives, the deepening of the law of value across the world capitalist economy, and the expanded commodification of natural resources as a global restructuring of farm production takes place. This has raised several political questions on the agrarian front which are connected with the peasant question.

For AL and K, all these are not aspects of a linear process, but form a dynamic, multi-faceted and contradictory set of patterns. The agrarian question appears to have lost the role that it played in the classical transitions, in building accumulation. But now its role has shifted in building global industrial capital. This becomes apparent the moment the question is reconfigured to the global context. While the process of globalization has brought more and more petty commodity producers under the law of value than before, the consequences of differentiation and pauperization are manifest now in more complex ways. The peasant question has not disappeared but re-emerged as the global peasant question with multiple sub-questions within it.

NOTES

1. Summarized from A. Haroon Akram-Lodhi and Cristobal Kay, "Agrarian Question: Unearthing Foundations" (Part I) in *The Journal of Peasant Studies*, Vol. 37, No. 1, January 2010, 177-202.
2. Summarized from Akram-Lodhi and Cristobal Kay's Surveying the Agrarian Question Part II.

REFERENCES

Akram-Lodhi, 2009. 'Modernizing Subordination? A South Asian Perspective on World Development Report 2008: Agriculture and Development', *The Journal of Peasant Studies*, 36 (3)611-20.

A. Haroon Akram-Lodhi and Cristóbel Kay, (2010). Surveying the Agrarian Question (Part 1): Unearthing Foundations, Exploring Diversity, *The Journal of Peasant Studies*, 37:1, 177-202.

A. Haroon Akram-Lodhi and Cristóbel Kay (2010). Surveying the Agrarian Question (Part 2): Current Debates and Beyond, *The Journal of Peasant Studies*, 37:2, 255-284.

Araghi, F., 2009. 'The Invisible Hand and the Invisible Foot: Peasants, Dispossession and Globalization' in Akram Lodhi and Cristobal Kay edited *Peasants and Globalization: Political Economy, Rural Transformation Threat to Farmers, Food and Environment*, Monthly Review Press, New York.

Foster, J.B., 2009. *The Ecological Revolution: Making Peace with the Planet.* New York: Monthly Review Press.

Bernstein, Henry, 1994. 'Agrarian Classes in Capitalist Development' in L. Sklain edited *Capitalism and Development*, Routledge, 99. 40-71.

Bernstein, Henry, 1996. 'Agrarian Question, Then and Now' *The Journal of Peasant Studies*, 24(1/2), 22-59.

Bernstein, Henry, 2006. 'Is There an Agrarian Question in the 21st Century?' *Canadian Journal of Development Studies*, 27(4) 446-60.

Brenner, R., 1977. 'The Origins of Capitalist Development : A Critique of Non-Smithian Marxism', *New Left Review*, 104, 25-92.

Blaike, P., 1985. *The Political Economy of Soil Erosion in developing Countries*, Longman, London.

Byres, T.J., 1996. *Capitalism from Above and From Below: Essay in Comparative Political Economy*, Macmillan, London.

Dobb, M., 1963. *Studies in the Development of Capitalism.* London: Routledge & Kegan Paul.

Hilton, R.H., 1976. Introduction. In: Paul Sweezy et al., eds. *The Transition from Feudalism to Capitalism.* London: Verso, pp. 9–29.

Hobsbawm, E.J., 1994. *Age of Extremes: The Short Twentieth Century,* 1914–1991. London: Michael Joseph.

Marx, K., 1976. *Capital: A Critique of Political Economy,* Vol. 1. Harmondsworth: Penguin Books. First Published in 1867.

McMichael, P., 2009. Food Sovereignty, Social Reproduction and the Agrarian Question, in A.H. Akram-Lodhi and C. Kay, eds. *Peasants and Globalization: Political Economy, Rural Transformation and the Agrarian Question.* London: Routledge, pp. 288–312.

Pearce, R., 1985. 'The Agrarian Question', in Z.G. Baranski and J.R. Short, eds. *Developing Contemporary Marxism*. London: Macmillan, pp. 58–85.

Sweezy, P., et al. 1976. *The Transition from Feudalism to Capitalism*. London: Verso.

Veltmeyer, H., 2006. Introduction: Development and the Agrarian Question. *Canadian Journal of Development Studies*, 27(4), 445–8.

Weis, T., 2007. *The Global Food Economy: The Battle for the Future of Farming*. London: Zed Press.

World Bank. 2007. *World Development Report 2008: Agriculture for Development*. Washington, DC: The World Bank.

11

Capital and Non-Capital in Capitalism in India[1]

[Kalyan Sanyal]

Background

The following ten-point framework of Marxist economic theory needs to be kept in mind in order to understand Kalyan Sanyal's argument:

1. Capital has a universalizing tendency, i.e. a tendency to make labour a universal identical commodity, i.e. it reduces all labour to a standard output fully exchangeable between one labourer and another. It does this concretely through mechanization of production, simplification of labour, stripping the labourer of all specific skills. It eliminates all relations of production in favour of the pure economic relation between the capitalist and wage-labourer.
2. Thus, capital tends to proletarianize, absorb and subjugate all labourers as sellers of a single identical form of unskilled wage labour. The theory of human labour as an abstract, simple commodity reflects the concrete lives of labourers stripped of all features.
3. Capitalism will swallow the entirety of social labour to meet its insatiable appetite for surplus value so that it is re-invested in industry.
4. Capitalism proposes a chimera of universal human rights (fundamentally to property) as the foundation of the

freedom of the individual to pursue wealth in its economic system. However, this bourgeois notion of a human right that is available to a few is based on the subjugation and exploitation of the unfreedom of most wage-labourers.

5. Capitalism begins its epoch with primitive accumulation which violently appropriates all forms of property, wealth, obligation and customary right that existed in the preceding (feudal) period.
6. Mature capital creates wealth for investment through the generation of surplus value within its own system. Primitive accumulation is left behind as a necessary transitional phase in the prehistory of capital.
7. This total absorption and uniform exploitation of wage labour will result in the proletariat which begins to think and act as a class-for-itself that recognizes its common interest and unity. Thus, the proletariat will be the first to conceive the true universality of society in the fundamental equality of its members.
8. The unequal distribution and concentration of wealth in mature capitalist society will also result in a crisis in political economy due to cyclical overproduction. This is matched by an impoverished proletariat that is unable to meet its needs, is conscious of its exploitation, and has a vision of equality which ultimately drives the proletarian revolution.
9. The revolution will in theory produce true universal right and well-being where all human beings can access what they need.
10. There are variations in this basic theoretical framework, especially with Gramsci, but in general the theory of transition and universalizing drive of capital are central to Marxist theory.

The problem with this universal theory of economic transformation is that it does not describe what happens in Third World nation states. Such a transition has also not occurred in many First World nation states. Theoretical studies of the economic transition (in relation to agriculture), especially in relation to

First World nation states, are being presented in other articles and summaries in this reader. This paper will deal with Kalyan Sanyal's own important critique of Indian Marxism's theoretical assumption of post-colonial economic transformation of feudal conditions of obligation into capitalist wage labour.

There have been several variants and theorizations within and after Marxism which try to deal with the complexity of the problem of capitalist transformation in Third World, postcolonial nation states. All these, Sanyal argues, depend on some underlying assumption that a capitalist transition takes place here too. Thus it is assumed that the labour force is absorbed into a universal exploitative relationship thus forming the basis for a proletarian transformation of Third World economies and societies. If the idea of a proletarian revolution has worn thin, there remains the hope/promise that the labour force will be fully absorbed and live a better life than under feudal conditions.

What would be the theoretical and practical implications if such a universal absorption and transition to capitalism does not occur?

First Observations

Sanyal quotes Ignacy Sachs' observation regarding Brazil's economic scenario, that

> ...Brazil was transformed into a BELINDA–a Belgium in the middle of an India, with parts of the [northeast] comparable to a Bangladesh. Industrialization had the opposite effect to that anticipated by Arthur Lewis. Instead of gradually exhausting the reserve of unskilled labour by drawing it into the modern organized sector, it deepened the process of *exclusion and social segregation*. It created a huge surplus of underemployed labour in the cities, including ... casual agricultural workers *expelled* from the rural areas by mechanization of large estates. (Sachs 1991: 99, cited in Sanyal 2007, emphasis Sanyal)

Sanyal suggests that there is a symptomatic, ugly stagnation of labour which is evident even in Indian cities and the countryside. This is best understood in a metaphor that refers to Michel Foucault's work on madness in the 16th century, where he described the (European) Ship of Fools carrying madmen drifting from port to port, touching each city while never allowing them to disembark or escape. This was Europe's way of expelling from society and yet keeping chained to its periphery its population of the 'insane', excluding, yet confining them. In Third World countries today, Sanyal argues, large populations are similarly kept apart from the development process. They are not absorbed as wage labour, yet not left alone to their devices, creating a large and permanent reserve army of the unemployed. Sanyal argues:

> Foregrounding of the phenomenon of exclusion and marginalization in the portrayal of the Third World economies, for me, is a representational strategy. My picture is very different from the way the economic formation of the Third World is represented in the dominant mainstream discourse of development. The mainstream discourse views underdevelopment as an initial condition waiting to be transformed in the process of modernization and development. It understands the persistence of underdevelopment as the reflection of insufficiency of development. This is seen as the inability of the modern sector to expand sufficiently and transmit its dynamic to the underdeveloped periphery; in other words, underdevelopment is the residual of the initial condition that the process of development fails to transform. (46-7, modified)

Having laid out the claim of the dominant discourse, Sanyal puts forward his own challenge to this view:

> In contrast to this, I see the representation of under-development in terms of castaways of development. I.e. I see underdevelopment resulting from the development process itself. This, to me, signals a new theoretical space in which a radically new conceptualization of the post-colonial economic formation is possible. Such a conceptualization brings to the fore the phenomenon of exclusion and confinement as an essential condition of capital's existence. It also makes visible the specific technology of power that helps create that condition. (47, modified)

Two questions need to be addressed: a) the theoretical implications of this perspective b) the practical mechanism of the process.

Theoretical Shifts

(a) In orthodox theory, primitive accumulation is, to recap, how early capital formation takes places. It is the process by which the pre-capitalist worker is "divorced from the means of production" (i.e. access to land, tools, skills, Marx 2010, 668). It is the process by which "great masses of men are suddenly and forcibly torn from their means of subsistence and hurled as free and 'unattached' proletarians on the labour-market". (ibid., 669). Primitive accumulation is the prehistory of capital. Once capital universalizes itself, primitive accumulation ceases to exist and all investment generation occurs through surplus labour within capital.

Sanyal's proposition is that at the post-colonial margin, metropolitan capital depends on continuous primitive accumulation. Capital never comes fully into being on its own. It is constantly transforming itself without completing the transition. Hence the process of primitive accumulation is a continuous process that happens alongside perpetual capital formation. In other words, agricultural workers are constantly expropriated, their resources taken from them and they are cast out of their places of subsistence.

(b) In orthodox theory, the workers who are expropriated are thrown, 'unattached' into the marketplace so that capital employs them as wage labour. This way, capital absorbs and exploits the expropriated workers, generating surplus value through this employment/exploitation. Capital also provides the socio-economic conditions of a universal exploitation that leads the proletariat to become conscious of its exploitation and develop a revolutionary consciousness as a being-for-itself.

Sanyal argues that in post-colonial development, those people thrown out of their traditional means of occupation are not absorbed. Thus, the possibility of wage labour as a means of subsistence after expropriation does not exist, and any development of their condition through proletarianization and progressive consciousness towards a being-for-self of the

> proletariat is not open to them. They are instead castaways who have no opportunity to enter the development process. They are thus excluded from development within the capitalist system.

The problem then is, how are these castaways maintained without being provided wage labour?

Practical Considerations

Sanyal argues that once the subsistence workers have been expropriated by primitive accumulation, they are completely at the mercy of the elements. There is no inherent reason why the expropriated must survive, and the history of early modern Europe has many examples of the dispossessed perishing in famines and epidemics. However, Sanyal continues, today it is no longer possible to let the jobless perish.

> Discourses of democracy and human rights have emerged and consolidated themselves to form an inescapable and integral part of the political and social order. As relatively autonomous discourses, they have constituted an environment within which capital has to reproduce itself. A crucial condition of that reproduction is that the victims of primitive accumulation be addressed in terms of what Michel Foucault has called "governmentality". These are interventions on the part of the developmental state (and non-state organizations) to promote the well-being of the population. What I identify as a reversal of primitive accumulation refers to this realm of welfarist governmentality; the creation of a need economy is an imperative of governance. (60, modified)

Thus, to support the expropriated, there must be a return flow of wealth from within capitalism to the outside, a reversal of the expropriation that is caused by primitive accumulation. Money thus flows out from the capitalist sector into the need sector, or the non-capital sector. This money is not in the circuit in which capital grows through reinvestment of surplus value. It is used by a non-capital need economy to sustain the expropriated through various marginalized forms of subsistence that do not contribute to capital. This reverse flow of capital occurs through the globally normative discourse and practice of development, which through state and non-state actors, channels and controls to an extent this reverse flow.

However, the moment any aspect of the need economy stabilizes and begins to grow through the normal processes of reinvestment, the capitalist economy will swoop down on these stabilized and growth-oriented aspects and dispossess or expropriate the successful actors.

It is for this reason Sanyal adopts the Ship of Fools metaphor to describe the marginalized who are neither left to exit the system nor allowed to integrate–they are excluded and held close simultaneously.

Implications

There are different implications of Sanyal's theoretical proposal:

- We can no longer look to capitalism to absorb all workers in its system thus creating a universal proletariat. There will always be the marginalized, eking out an existence, surviving on a minimal transfer of resources from the state to non-capital. Trademark slums and other tell-tale signs of dire impoverishment will remain part of the postcolonial landscape.
- The proletariat no longer has the potential to become a consciousness-for-itself which can represent a true universal human good. If the capitalism does not absorb all labour and permits the existence of an army of the unemployed at the margin, a proletarian consciousness cannot be universal since even below them exist the permanent reserve army of the unemployed, who have no means to unite, no common ground to fight their battles against capital, which is from that point of view an unseen enemy.
- Capitalism is not an autonomous system, and is regulated by a state/non-state governmental process. If capitalism does not absorb the entire labouring population, it can no longer function fully autonomously as a base upon which the

superstructure of the state, law, education and other welfare institutions will rest. The state has to be a referee between capital and non-capital and will thus be beyond the grip of capital, and the latter's hegemony will be compromised. This will mean that the state will offer a means to direct the functioning of capital to a degree.

- The notion of a socio-economic transition through the force of a dialectic and through a process of sublated contradictions no longer holds. Once a marginalized population exists, the dynamics of the proletariat will not function and the process of a revolutionary transformation will not have its driving force.
- However, the autonomous structure of non-capital's will to survive may frame a different form of a consciousness-for-itself of the marginalized unemployed. This is because there will be other modes of organization or conscientization that may open out as possibilities for the marginalized, and such new possibilities will dictate the forms of development of non-capital in the era of capitalism (and perhaps beyond).
- What the future holds is no longer clear, but is open to intervention and modification. This is because the internal dynamic of the Marxist dialectic, whereby the proletariat begins to represent consciousness of society as a whole, from the perspective of the exploited, cannot work. The proletarian consciousness is no longer the lowest one in the hierarchy. It cannot imagine an exploitation that is below slavery—exploitation of the very possibility of employment through denial.

NOTE

1. This is a summary of the theoretical position developed by Kalyan Sanyal, *Rethinking Capitalist Development: Primitive Accumulation, Governmentality and Postcolonial Capitalism,* (New Delhi: Routledge, 2007).

12

Transition in Indian Agriculture: What Does the Data Tell Us?[1]

[Amit Basole and Deepankar Basu]

Basole and Basu set out to understand the nature of exploitation of labour and appropriation of surplus in the Indian economy. Given the transitional nature of the Indian economy from feudalism where the appropriation and exploitation is direct, to capitalism where it occurs in a totally concealed manner, through the institution of wage labour, assessing the nature of exploitation becomes crucial to understand the political and social implications. Can this assessment be purely theoretical? Basole and Basu argue that it has to be empirical. They examine some key structural features of Indian agriculture to arrive at an assessment. For them, focus on agriculture and informal industry is crucial because most scholars agree on the prevalence of capitalist relations of production in the 'formal' sector. Such an empirical assessment, they note is important to assess the character of capitalist development in India.

How do they undertake this assessment? They build their argument on the basis of NSS data, from different rounds, both at aggregate level and also at the state level, related to agrarian structure, employment, tenancy, credit, and sources of income of the working masses in agriculture. Each of the following sections discusses in detail what such data suggests about capitalist transition in agriculture in India. The authors examine the class structure at the all-India level on the basis of the following factors: size of landholdings; ownership at the state level; types of tenancy; owner-

tenant relationships; extent of landlessness; sources of livelihood in the rural areas; surplus accumulation; nature of dominant class.

1. Decline in the Share of Agriculture in the Indian Economy

A typical modern capitalist economy experiences what economists call 'structural transformation', constituting a) declining share of income from agriculture and b) workers dependent on agriculture in the national economy. In India, the first part is achieved, leaving a huge gap in the latter. The share of agricultural GDP declined sharply from 56 per cent in 1950 to about 14 per cent in 2011 owing to the relative faster growth of the non-agricultural sector. As a result, agriculture as a sector as a whole commands far less economic power. Yet, the share of labour force engaged in agriculture fell from 68 per cent to only 49 per cent during the same time. Such a large workforce still engaged in agriculture reflects, Basole and Basu note, lack of opportunities outside agriculture.

Thus, the share of GDP contributed by agriculture has steadily declined over the last five decades; this decline has not been matched by a decline in the share of the workforce engaged in agriculture. This renders a large section of rural workers confined to low productive work and low income.

2. Increase in the Number of Marginal and Small Farmer Households

What is happening to those engaged in agriculture? Normally, with capitalist transition, one may expect, though it is not certain, an increase in average landholding size. Contrarily, in Indian agriculture, the average size of ownership holdings has declined from about 2.01 acres in 1961 to 0.81 acres in 2003. Same pattern of monotonic decline is also observed in operational holdings.

Next, they look at changes in agrarian structure in terms of holding size. NSS classifies agricultural holdings into five categories, namely, marginal farmer as one holding land less than 1 hectare, small 1-2 ha; semi-medium 2-4 ha; medium 4-10 ha; and large as holding more than 10 ha. In the last 60 years, among these size-classes, the proportion of marginal and small households has increased steadily from about 75 per cent of all rural households in 1961 to 90 per cent in 2003. This rather large increase in the share of marginal/small farmers has been matched by a steady decline of large, medium and semi-medium farmers. Large and medium farmer households together comprise a minuscule 3.6 per cent of total rural households in rural India today, down from 12 per cent in 1961. Between the decline in the share of large landholding families and the increase in the share of marginal farmer families, the "small" farmer family has managed to more or less maintain its share constant over the past five decades, increasing marginally from 9 per cent to 11 per cent of all rural households between 1961 and 2003.

Thus, the average size of agricultural holdings, both ownership and operational, has seen a steady decline over the last five decades, with the average ownership holding in 2002-03 being 0.73 hectares.

3. Increase in the Area Owned by Small and Marginal Farmers

They point out that the area operated by these respective size classes also shows a similar trend. The share of total area owned by marginal and small farmers has steadily increased from 8 per cent of total area in 1961 to about 23 per cent in 2003. The share of area owned by large farmer households declined from 28 per cent in 1961 to about 12 per cent in 2003; the corresponding share owned by "medium" households declined from 31 per cent in 1961 to about 23 per cent in 2003. Caught between these two trends is the semi-medium farmer family which has kept its share in the total area owned more or less constant since 1971 at around 20 per cent.

The share of land owned by large and medium holding families has steadily declined over the last few decades from around 60 per cent to 34 per cent which indicates their declining economic, social and political power in rural areas. The share of marginal, small and semi-medium holdings has increased from around 31 per cent to

80 per cent indicates proliferation of a large class of powerless petty landowners.

4. Continuing Inequality in Ownership of Land

This changing structure of land ownership, they point out, has not made distribution any more equitable. The Gini coefficient, a measure of inequality, of ownership distribution, from being 0.73 in 1961-62, remained the same, marginally increasing to 0.74 in 2003 (GOI, 2006). Even the average size of the large holding is about 67 times that of the marginal holding in 2003; 27 times that of medium holding. This occurred due to the simultaneous reduction in the size of the small landholdings along with the large landholdings.

Such a skewed distribution of land ownership of course in itself, they note, is not very useful to understand the dominant relations of production and modes of surplus extraction most in use. A feudal mode of production can have as much skewed distribution as a capitalist mode of production. While it is true that class power and landholding size need not exactly match, it may still serve as a useful indicator to approximate the class power, because those who have larger holdings are also likely to own more animals, implements, and machinery. Hence size classes can be taken to as a proxy for class power.

Therefore the ownership of land remained as unequal as it was five decades ago which indicates that the class dominance has also remained the same.

5. Which States Have Larger Number of Large Landholdings?

State-level comparisons are essential, given the wide variation in historical and geographical conditions in India. For analytical convenience, Basole and Basu divide all the states into two groups. The first group consists of those with the largest share of area by large farmers. Such "large landholding states" are: Andhra Pradesh, Gujarat, Haryana, Karnataka, Madhya Pradesh, Maharashtra, Punjab, and Rajasthan. The second group of states are those with a relatively small proportion of area held by large farmers or the "small landholding states": Assam, Bihar, Himachal Pradesh, Jammu and Kashmir, Kerala, Odisha, Tamil Nadu, Uttar Pradesh, and West Bengal.

As also suggested by micro-studies, the first group of states with large landholding is also associated with a relatively higher growth of capitalist relations of production in agriculture; the second group consists of the states which are still encumbered by remnants of pre-capitalist modes of organizing production. But even here, there has been a decline in the share of land owned by large farmers. This suggests that the economic position commanded by semi-feudal landlords appears to have declined relative to the rich middle peasants and capitalist landlords at the national, state and regional level. The semi-feudal landlords seem to have been replaced by rich middle peasants as the ruling bloc in the agrarian structure of contemporary India.

Thus, more developed and big (irrigation and income-wise) states have less fragmentation of holdings, like Andhra Pradesh, Gujarat, Haryana, Karnataka, Madhya Pradesh, Maharashtra, Punjab and Rajasthan. However, states like Assam, Bihar, Himachal Pradesh, J&K, Kerala, Odisha, Tamil Nadu, Uttar Pradesh and West Bengal have more fragmentation.

6. How Many People Continue to be Landless?

Proletarianization, an important indicator of development of capitalist economy, is reflected in the extent of landlessness. According to (NSSO) data, the extent of landlessness in Indian agriculture has stayed more or less constant over the last five decades: at 11.7 per cent in 1961 which marginally declined to 10 per cent in 2003. If those owning land less than 0.2 ha are added, it stands at 44 per cent in 2003, if one uses 0.4 ha as a threshold, then it increases to 60 per cent. The poorest rural households, who are effectively landless, own only 6 per cent of the land used for cultivation. The largest share of landless households are prevalent in Himachal Pradesh, Maharashtra and Karnataka; and the smallest share in states like Jammu & Kashmir, Kerala, Punjab, Rajasthan, Uttar Pradesh and West Bengal.

The relative share and absolute number of cultivators in total agricultural workers has decreased in the past one decade. At all India level, the number of cultivators, which increased between 1961-81 from 79 to 121 million, remained constant at 125 million between 1991 and 2001, but reversed during 2001-2011, to fall below 102 million for the first time suggesting about 23 million cultivators have quit agriculture between 1991-2011. A fall in cultivator number should mean they are diversifying either into the non-farm sector as producers of various kinds or workers.

Thus, the effective landlessness (by including those who have 0.29 ha or 0.73 acres) is quite large to an extent of 60 per cent in 2002-03.

7. Declining Tenancy

Growing landlessness may not itself suggest proletarianization where tenancy is widely prevalent. There are after all, two different ways in which the surplus labour is appropriated by the ruling classes, one directly as wage-labour and second indirectly as land rent. The first source is clearly associated with capitalist relations, while the second could be associated with semi-feudal methods of surplus extraction.

Aggregate level data from NSSO (and also from the Agricultural Census) suggests a sharp decline in the share of tenant households, from 25 per cent in 1971-72 to 12 per cent in 2003; the percentage of area leased in total area owned has too declined from 12 per cent in 1971-72 to 7 per cent in 2003. Such decline of tenancy is also observed for operational holdings.

The share of operational holdings with partly or wholly leased-in land has fallen drastically from around 24 per cent in 1960-61 to 10 per cent in 2002-03. In terms of the total area operated, the percentage share of area leased in has declined from 10.7 per cent in 1960-61 to 6.5 per cent in 2003. This indicates a gradual shift from tenant cultivation to self-cultivation.

Among size classes, while there is an increase in the share of large tenancy holdings, which increased from 9.5 per cent to 13.5 per cent during 1961-2001, but area leased-in by them declined from 8.3 to 6.1 per cent. For all other classes, shares of tenancy holdings in total holdings and their respective shares in land leased-in also declined.

How consistent is this trend across states? The states with area under tenancy increased are Andhra Pradesh, Gujarat, Odisha, Kerala, and Punjab. Except in Punjab, the area is less than 10 per cent. In all other states, the share of tenant holdings and area leased has significantly reduced. This means that tenancy is increasing in states where the hold of semi-feudal relations is already weakened.

To conclude, share of tenant holdings, as per the NSS data, declined drastically in the last five decades, area from 24 to 10 per cent. The area under tenancy also drastically declined. While sharecropping–that house pre-capitalist relations held on, in the other areas fixed rent contracts reflecting commercial character is on the rise.

8. Are Current Forms of Tenancy Feudal or Capitalist?

Thus, states which are usually considered to be the bastions of semi-feudal and pre-capitalist production relations are not the ones which have the highest prevalence of tenancy, with the exception of Odisha. It seems, therefore, that the development of capitalism in Indian agriculture has peculiarly used tenancy and other forms of pre-capitalist relations of production as the means of reducing the costs of production and controlling labour.

Further, in order to understand the nature of tenancy, one should look at types of tenancy contracts. Fixed cash or kind rent which indicate more capitalist relation; whereas sharecropping can involve semi-feudal relations. As per the NSS data, the area under sharecopping has not changed much over time which stood at around 40 per cent, while informal commercial leasing on kind and cash rent has increased from 38 to 50 per cent during 1961-2003.

In Haryana and Punjab, which have the largest share of leased-in land, the predominant type of tenancy is fixed money lease contracts. Poorer states like Assam, Bihar, Odisha and Uttar

Pradesh, have sharecropping as a predominant form of tenancy contract. This difference is important because the form of tenancy is radically different in the two groups of states.

In states like Punjab and Haryana, tenant cultivators are not the landless and poor peasants; it is rather the middle and rich peasants who lease-in land to increase the size of their agricultural operations and reap some economies of scale on their capital investments. The fixed money rent form of tenancy is no indicator of pre-capitalist relations, but is very much a capitalist development in agriculture. In states like Bihar and Odisha, on the other hand, tenancy is still predominantly of the old form, where the largest group of lessees is landless and near-landless peasants. In such a scenario, sharecropping operates as a semi-feudal mode of surplus extraction, where land rent can be considered as pre-capitalist rent.

Tenancy in certain states is capitalist, where the landed peasants lease–in land to reap economies of scale on their capital investments. In other states, tenancy is in the old form where it operates in the semi-feudal mode of surplus extraction and is pre-capitalist in form.

9. Wage Labour and Family Labour: Which is Feudal and Which is Capitalist?

Sources of income in the self employment category include implicit wage for family labour, proceeds from trading and finance. All these reflect capitalist relations (mainly variations on the putting-out system), but are of a different nature; hence non-wage income can often mask the underlying capitalist relations.

Similarly, wage income can often mask prevalence of 'unfree' labour relations. Many of these "unfree" relations, for example institution of annual farm labour, are created by capitalism and are not relics of a pre-capitalist past. In addition, often the same individual participates in several types of economic activities, requiring us to distinguish between wage and non-wage income at micro-level. With these caveats, Basole and Basu proceed to study the sources of rural income since the aggregate level distinction between wage and non-wage income still has important clues to offer about the relations of production in India.

With a preponderant share of petty commodity producers among those in agriculture who derive their income from farm activity as well as wage labour, it is important to look at sources of income for farm households. Which is the dominant source? A predominance of wage income would suggest an increasing proletarian character; but a continued dependence on income from cultivation would suggest an unclear story. At the same time non-wage income source need not imply pre-capitalist relations.

Finally, small agricultural holdings are unviable, dependence on these keeps the rural households in perpetual indebtedness and pauperization.

10. Which is More: Wage Income or Income from Cultivation?

Small size of the holding, which is a serious problem in India, generally leads to low farm income. Existence of the ground-rent barrier, lack of formal credit, dwindling rural public investment, eroding irrigation and exploitative input markets all contribute to this low income. As data indicates, the average profit per hectare from cultivation (excluding value of family labour or rent of owned land), was Rs. 6756 for Kharif and Rs. 9290 for the Rabi season in 2003. Such low level of income compels most rural families to supplement incomes through wage labour with petty commodity production in both the agricultural and non-agricultural sector.

NSS data on different sources of rural income by the size-class of ownership holdings suggests that, first, it is only among the rural families with more than 4 hectares of land total farm that income exceeds average expenditure. If one remembers that 96 per cent of rural households owned less than 4 hectares in 2003, farm incomes for 96 per cent of rural households come from cultivation, wage labour and petty production. Second, for a large majority of 60 per cent of farm households, the primary source of income is wage income, not cultivation, which provided more than 50 per cent of their total monthly income in 2003. Landless households anyway depend on wage income. Third, income from petty commodity production accounts for 20 per cent of the total income for about 80 per cent of rural households in 2003.

Thus aggregate level data suggests that wage income has become the most important source of income for the majority of the rural population. This implies that surplus extraction through the institution of wage-labour has become the dominant form of extracting the surplus product of direct producers. Income from petty commodity production being as low as 20 per cent indicates the exploitation of this large section by merchant capital through unequal exchange.

In spite of a large number of rural families owning small parcels of land, their major source of income now is wage income, almost up to 60 per cent. Only 20 per cent of their income comes from cultivation, which reflects the exploitation in agricultural markets. The remaining 20 per cent is from other petty activities.

11. Why Do Informal and Formal Credit Services Decline or Increase?

Unregulated informal credit market operated by usurious capital gets a larger share in surplus labour without participating in its generation hence is necessarily parasitic. Informal credit often operates through inter-linkages in product and labour markets, which facilitate extraction of surplus through unequal exchange. It is the small peasantry which is often the biggest victims of these. Has the share of those dependent on informal money-lender class really changed?

NSS rounds suggest that the share of total rural credit provided by moneylenders declined substantially between 1961 and 1981 from 70 per cent to 18 per cent of total credit. This is a huge decrease! However, moneylenders seem to have made a comeback in the 1980s. Their share went up to 28 per cent. A new class of moneylenders replaced the older class of landlords. Now various groups of the rural population, like traders, school teachers, government servants, lawyers, rich farmers, and other members of the petty bourgeois class, have entered this lucrative business, facilitated by the gradual but steady retreat of formal credit institutions.

Among the states, other than five states of Punjab, Rajasthan, Assam, Bihar and Andhra Pradesh, all the other states have a higher proportion of formal credit in 2003. Second, some of the states with relatively well developed capitalist agriculture like Punjab, Andhra Pradesh and Tamil Nadu also have a higher prevalence of informal credit. In Punjab, for instance, one of the main players in the informal credit market is the trader-middleman known as the *adtidar* or the commission agent who often provides credit, sells inputs and also procures the output from the farmer. This typical pattern of interlinked markets allows the surplus product to be easily extracted from the direct producer through unequal exchange whereby input prices are inflated and output prices depressed. Interestingly, West Bengal, which has had some limited degree of land reforms in the past, also shows a high percentage of non-institutional forms of rural credit.

Thus, there is a reasonably high growth of formal credit market, which caters to 70 per cent of farm investment. While this disproportionately goes to large and medium farmers, smaller peasants remain dependent on informal moneylenders.

12. Capital Formation or Investment in Agriculture

An important question relating to the development of capitalist relations of production in Indian agriculture is whether there has been any significant trend towards reinvestment of surplus and capital accumulation in the agrarian economy. Lack of capital formation in agriculture would indicate production relations hindering the development of productive forces. Aggregate level data on gross capital formation in Indian agriculture shows interesting temporal patterns. The gross value of capital stocks has more than tripled in real terms (1993-94 prices) over the last four decades, moving from Rs. 63,000 crores in 1961 to Rs. 1,90,000 crores in 1999.

For the period 1961-99, gross capital formation in agriculture (GCFA) grew at about 3 per cent per annum, a significant rate of growth by developing country standards. GCFA grew at 5.05 per cent in 1960s, 8.7 per cent in the 1970s; thereafter, it slowed down at -0.33 per cent in the 1990s. It again picked up to 2.8 per cent in the 1990s. The slowdown in capital formation is largely due to deceleration of public sector capital expenditures in agriculture. Since 1993, however, the private capital expenditure, increased at a whopping 16.7 per cent (Gulati and Bathla, 2002). The data suggests two things, investment or capital formation in agriculture significantly increased in the 1970s and 1980s, spearheaded by the state investment. After the reforms, a decline in public investment is more than outweighed by private investment in agriculture.

There was a significant capital accumulation in the agricultural sector during the 1970-90s that enabled a long-term growth of output at a growth rate of 2.7 per cent, This capital formation was led initially by the public sector share, and then by private investment after 1991.

Over the past few decades, the relations of production in the Indian agrarian economy have slowly evolved from "semi-feudal" towards "capitalist". The predominant mode of surplus extraction seems to be through the institution of wage-labour, the defining feature of capitalism. Articulated to the global capitalist-imperialist system, the development of capitalism in the periphery has not led to the growth of income and living standards of the vast majority of the rural population. Two main forms of surplus appropriation from producers seem to exist (a) through wage-labour, and (b) unequal exchange value appropriation from petty producers through interlocked markets with monopolistic institutions. The process of class differentiation is slowed down in the long chain connecting the Indian economy to the global capitalist system, which sustains a large "informal" production sector, organized by petty commodity production, both of agricultural and non-agricultural commodities. Preponderance of this class impedes development of proletarian class consciousness and complicated the task of revolutionary politics.

NOTE

1. 'Summary of Relations of Production and Modes of Surplus Extraction in India: Part I Agriculture' by Amit Basole and Deepankar Basu, *Economic and Political Weekly*, Vol. 46, Issue No. 14, April 2, 2011.

REFERENCE

Amit Basole and Deepankar Basu, (2011), 'Relations of Production and Modes of Surplus Extraction in India: Part I Agriculture', *Economic and Political Weekly*, April 2, Vol. xlvi, No. 14, pp. 41-56.

13

The Agrarian Question Under Neoliberalism and Land Reforms in India[1]

[Jens Lerche]

This paper interrogates the positions on the agrarian question in India, to reach fresh conclusions about important agrarian policies of the Left, including that of land reforms. Internationally, the classical political economy approach to agrarian transitions has been challenged by positions arguing (a) that neoliberalism and the international corporate food regime have led to a new dominant contradiction between the peasantry and multinational agribusiness or (b) that the agrarian question for capital has been bypassed. It is shown that most analyses of the agrarian question in India, including those of the Indian Left parties, tend to adhere either to the classical political economy approach, or their analyses are close to the peasantry versus the corporate food regime approach. In spite of this, it is here argued that an empirical analysis of agrarian transition in India lends credence to some aspects of the third position; that is, the argument that the agrarian question for capital has been bypassed.

Introduction

Even though the modes of production debate in India took place in the 1970s, its influence on the approach and the political stances of the Indian Left on agrarian issues are still rooted in the analyses of that time. Granted, the Indian neoliberal turn, a few decades ago, led to substantial changes in ground realities and that continue to occur, it would be shown that it needs at least one very radical rethink. But many core characteristics of the analyses and policy perspectives remain the same. This includes, in various guises, the characterization of the capitalist development of Indian agriculture as encompassing semi-feudal features; and a focus on land reforms as a main policy strategy to modernize agriculture and significantly strengthen the political and economic position of poor peasants and agricultural workers. This paper reviews the various positions in the present debate on agrarian questions relating to India, to reach fresh conclusions about important agrarian policies of the Left, including that of land reforms.

That said, as pointed out by Utsa Patnaik (1986), the modes of production debate remained a theoretical cul-de-sac. As argued by her, it is more useful to return to the classical 'agrarian questions' approach, which goes back at least to 1949 among the Indian left (Namboodiripad 1949). Internationally, there has been a renewed attention on the agrarian questions approach within agrarian political economy studies during the past 20 years. This paper, by mapping the important stand-points in literature, re-interrogates the various positions in the Indian debate on the agrarian question in India, to reach fresh conclusions about important agrarian policies of the Left, including that of land reforms.

Agrarian Questions

It is useful to start from the concrete meanings that Terence Byres suggested of the agrarian question in poor countries (Byres 1986, 1991, 1996) that the continuing existence of substantive obstacles in the countryside of the poor countries to an unleashing of the forces capable of generating economic development, both inside and outside agriculture. It represents a failure of accumulation to proceed adequately in the countryside–that impinging powerfully upon the town; an intimately related failure of class formation in the countryside, appropriate to that accumulation; and a failure of the state to mediate successfully those transitions which we may encapsulate as the agrarian transition (Byres 1995, 509). Byres' positions are influenced by two important sources, one from

Preobrazensky's work on socialist accumulation in the Soviet Union in 1926 and the experience of Indian planning where an annual growth of 5 per cent for agriculture was necessary for creation of surplus that could be transferred to investment in the modern sector modelled on the Lewis Model of Development. Throughout his comparative studies, Byres has argued that successful agrarian transitions led to dynamic national capitalist development, and that blocked agrarian transition did the opposite. The nature and timing of each successful (and each failed) agrarian transition must be understood as a result of the specific agrarian class struggle, driven by the nature of the landlord class, class struggle and peasant differentiation. (Byres 2009, 34). He further added nuances to Lenin's approach to locate two paths of agrarian change–'from above' and 'from below', are inadequate in themselves to understand the significant differences between the existing transformations (Byres 1991, 1996)[2].

Byres' focus on the necessity of agrarian transformation for overall capitalist development also leads to a strong view on land reforms. According to him, land reforms may be conceptualized either from a social justice perspective or from a productivity perspective. However 'just' they may seem in the short term, redistributive land reforms leading to very small farm sizes are counterproductive when seen from the angle of the need for an 'unleashing of the forces capable of generating economic development'. Small sized farms hamper development of productive agriculture and hence are an obstacle to a proper agrarian transition. It is well known that after introduction of modernization in agriculture, the old-fashioned negative relation between holding-size and productivity had also vanished. (Dyer 2004; Rakshit 2011).[3]

Byres' view on redistributive land reforms is an optimistic view of development that sees the transition to a high-growth capitalist economy as both historically progressive and also as potentially leading to better conditions for the erstwhile peasants. They may, eventually, find a better future in the modern non-agricultural economy than what is offered by farming miniature plots within a stagnant and backward agrarian economy.

However, Byres' 'classical' position on agrarian change as a process of transformation of agriculture, designed to contribute to capitalist industrialization through accumulation, differentiation and labour exploitation, faces two serious challengers, McMichael and Bernstein. Both argue that present-day capitalist development, especially under neoliberal globalization, must lead to a rethink of the agrarian question. However, they differ substantively in what such a rethink should entail. McMichael and others suggest that today, the main agrarian issue is the struggle by 'the peasantry' against the international corporate food regime, while Bernstein argues, from a position within agrarian political economy, that the 'agrarian question of capital' has been bypassed.

The first challenge is by McMichael and others to the political economy of the agrarian question is that the peasantry is incorporated into the global corporate food chain, in which peasantry, small and big, as a whole is subordinated[4]. Differentiation of peasantry is no longer an issue. Land reforms are welcome as a way to increase communitarian democracy. The crux of the battle lies in dealing with ecologically unfriendly corporate methods of farming, which immiserizes the peasantry on one hand and damages the ecology of agriculture on the other. To fight the global corporate clout, the peasantry becomes the radical political class. (McMichael 2008, 224). The question of economic feasibility of small farms loses attention under the concern for the larger peasant crisis affected by the corporate control over the production process. Apart from the differences with this selective anti-food-corporate regime perspective, it does address two issues that classical agrarian thinking are yet to deal with: first, extreme subordination of small-scale agrarian production to international capital in the era of neoliberal globalization; and, second, in its insistence that it is necessary to think of alternatives to economic growth based on fossil fuels.

The second challenge is posed by Henry Bernstein to the idea of resolution of the agrarian question under neoliberalism. Bernsetein argues that the agrarian question needs to be split into two different but related questions, one agrarian question of capital and two, agrarian question of labour.[5] Classical agrarian question of capital formulation rests on the assumption that there always exists a pre-capitalist agrarian sector and transformation of specific characteristics in it as necessary for accumulation in agriculture to begin with, and to supplement the accumulation in industry thereon. Bernstein argues that such a condition is either solved or bypassed by globalization of capital (Bernstein 2006, 450–1). Therefore, in today's world, the classical agrarian question has lost its traditional relevance; it needs a fresh look.

There are two issues here. First, Bernstein asserts that all forms of peasant production, including landlord dominated production systems are transformed into petty commodity producers and capitalist farmers, by the end of colonialism. The 'generalized commodity production' in agriculture is already created (Bernstein 2006, 454). Second, closed economy conditions necessary for home market-based capitalism, which rests on strong internal agriculture-industry relations are also altered. The globalization process reintegrated commodity markets and circuits of capital. Capital, even in a poor country, no longer necessarily depends on agrarian surplus, but can access global sources. Moreover, the state under neoliberal globalization lacks a will to mediate an arduous agrarian transformation for the sake of national capital, as it ceased to be *sine qua non* for the latter. Moreover, the increased global trade in agriculture and industry within the south has increased considerable interdependence in product and financial markets; building national intersectoral linkages is no longer necessary.

For the agrarian question of labour, land reform was considered important in classical understanding, since it not only makes small peasant farming commercially viable by assigning them economic holdings[6]; but also raises the rural wage rates and sustains aggregate demand for the non-agricultural sector. The growing non-farm sector would absorb the surplus labour. This would draw support from the bourgeoisie in the larger interest. This is often referred as the resolution of the agrarian question 'from below'. However, under the globalized regime land reform is no longer an attainable goal that can unite capital and peasants in a quest to create peasant-based growth and accumulation from below. Thereby, land reforms are off the policy agenda today. Bernstein argues that the agrarian question 'from below' has been replaced by the general question of the relationship between capital and labour. All classes of peasant producers are already transformed into capitalist or petty commodity producers. Petty commodity production entails the self-exploitation of family labour, often failing to get a 'generalized living wage'. The transformation that already ensued created 'different classes' of reserve army of labour, obliterating the pre-capitalist agrarian classes. For all classes of labour, irrespective of whether or not they have a foothold in the rural economy, the main problem is how to engage in struggles for improved conditions as footloose labour. As part of this, land reforms might help towards subsistence by way of providing farm plots, even if miniature in size (Bernstein 2006, 2007), even if this might be politically frustrating to achieve. However, what is noteworthy, since the agrarian question for capital has been bypassed and hence the quest for the formation of a highly productive agrarian sector is no longer on the cards, is that the objection to land reforms on grounds of reduced productivity is trumped by the social justice argument.

The Positions of the Indian Left

What is the broad academic and political position on India's agrarian transition? Interestingly, most of the views hark back to the modes of production debate. Party programmes of three major communist parties are considered here, which remained by and large unrevised for a long time, for example, Communist Party of India (Marxist) replaced its 1964 programme in 2000, Communist Party of India CPI-ML (Maoist-PWG) replaced its 1970 programme in 2004, so did MCCI (Maoist Communist Centre India)

In the academic opinion, Alice Thorner took the position that Indian agriculture came to be dominated by capitalist relations by the late 1970s (Thorner 1982, 2063). Utsa Patnaik held the view that despite peasant/landlord capitalism taking place in terms of wage labour exploitation, mechanization and market surplus, the nature of this capitalism is still perverse with 'built-in' depressors. This is so, because, landlords are unlikely to invest in agriculture unless profits exceed ground rents. Further, surplus expropriation uses pre-capitalist institutions such as caste-based and non-economic means. The overall nature of this capitalism, therefore, is 'semi-feudal' (Patnaik 1972, 1986). This meant that Indian agrarian capitalism is incapable to deliver a growth necessary to lift the rural masses out of poverty.

Two things are little unclear, first how unproductive are the activities of landlords or rich peasants, and the second, given the uneven development and varying forms of landlordism, there are no caveats provisioned for a general party programme. However, an overall dynamic of capitalist development is seen to drive a deep wedge between the rural rich: 'the landlords, capitalist farmers, rich peasants and their allies' on one hand and 'the mass of the rural poor: agricultural workers, poor peasants and the artisans' on the other. This development has been exacerbated by the liberalization in agriculture since 1991 and the entry of multinational corporations (MNCs) into agricultural commodity trading in the countryside (CPM 2008).

Assessing the impact of neoliberalism on the agrarian classes, the party congress in 2008 stated that land acquisitions for SEZs, mining, hydro projects, are leading to displacement and dispossession of rural poor. A worker-peasant alliance is sought to be built against bourgeoisie-landlord alliance in an 'anti-feudal, anti-monopoly and anti-imperialist struggle. Except the class of ex-landlords, the party document mentions, all other rural agrarian classes as victims of neoliberal globalization within the worker-peasant alliance. The land reform redux still forms the core objective of the 'people's democracy', which can be achieved by abolishing landlordism through radical land redistribution, along with demands for greater social security and opposition to liberalization, and MNCs.

While the vision to establish 'people's democracy' remains by far abstract, but the party's 2008 resolution includes specific demands like implementation of the recommendations of the National Commission of Farmers' (headed by M.S. Swaminathan), importantly to allocate 1 hectare of land to all landless households, and increase farm prices basis of 50 per cent over full cost (CPM 2008). The website of the party by 2011 lists an omnibus of issues like inflation, food security, rural employment guarantee (NREGA) and comprehensive social security legislation. CPM's overall understanding follows a classical line as those outlined by Byres, to aid the poor and middle peasant against parasitic landlords, help capitalist developments from within the peasantry and fight imperialism at the same time.

However, CPM's analysis about the necessity of reforms is at variance with the classical agrarian transition approach. Without being able to give an economic holding in the land redistribution, the goal of transferring efficiency holding to small producers is unlikely to be achieved. However, even if not serving deepening the goal of capitalist development, it may still be justified as a social justice goal.

Further more extreme left wing parties like CPI-ML (Maoists), also known as Naxalites, the understanding is indeed no different from the CPM fundamentally, except that they deny any salient capitalist development taking place in agriculture. They resolutely term the nature of the development as semi-feudal, since the landlords (neo-rich or ex-) siphon-off their surplus to unproductive activities; use traditional caste relations for appropriating the surplus. Further, the nature of capital in industry is comprador/semi-colonial, continues its historic parasitic existence on imported technologies, rendering itself incapable of significant accumulation. The overall nature of the capital is, therefore ruling classes in semi-feudal/comprador. The fight is to be waged against landlordism (cultural institutions of religion, caste, gender) and imperialism, including the current phase of neoliberalism [CPI(ML) 2007]. Land redistribution is seen to lie at the centre of all in fighting the primary contradiction in the society against feudal lords. A second 'basic' contradiction is between 'imperialism and the Indian people'. The targets of the revolution 'are the imperialists, the comprador bureaucratic bourgeoisie and the big landlord classes'.

Redistributive land reforms are necessary for democratizing socio-economic conditions; but again, it is only the landlords (and religious institutions) that should lose land. There is a minimal room for nuance here, they do not acknowledge that capitalist relations have made inroads into the countryside, compared to the CPI(M)'s analysis–the CPI(Maoist) characterization of semi-feudalism emphasizes the feudal structure much more than its partial transformation. With regard to neoliberalism, there is a tendency to view it as undifferentiated in its impact, and hence a hope to unite all the classes of people against it.

Like Patnaik (2005) argued that neoliberal policies have seriously hurt the country's food security, both from the supply as well as demand side. She observes a drastic fall in per capita net foodgrain availability, due to stagnation in productivity and fall in acreage under foodgrains, all resulting from reduction of farm subsidies, diversification into non-food crops, stagnation in food grain prices due to falling rural incomes. She drops her earlier emphasis on land question and peasant differentiation and declares peasantry as a whole is at the receiving end from globalization. In her later paper, she further elaborates it as a new phase of primitive accumulation where advanced nations have subsumed the peasantry under capital through contract farming, diverting land into biofuel production, resulting in a food crisis (Patnaik 2010 Sundarayya Memorial Lecture). In effect, Patnaik, moves closer to McMichael's position that all social classes have the common enemy, i.e. corporate food regime. And substitution of 'differentiation' with 'pauperization' is a departure from the classical agrarian question in the Marxian tradition.

The difficult question is whether her interpretation of the consequences of neoliberal globalization really holds true. Has the role played by the landlord class been reversed? Has peasant differentiation been superseded by peasant pauperization? Are the living standards falling; and does this warrant a new, non-class-specific development strategy, based on rejection of globalization and a turn towards a new type of national inward-orientated strategy based on small-scale production?

The perspective suggested by Bernstein that the agrarian question of capital has been bypassed, does not figure in the Indian debate. The evidence is that the agrarian question has lost much of its importance for capital in India. It is a fact the Indian agriculture could not produce robust growth and accumulation expected to provide for the industrial growth, in spite of introduction of new technology, nor did the agrarian bourgeoisie provide a major market for non-agricultural produce. Since the mid-1980s, India's growth momentum is sustained by the service sector, which provided stronger linkages to industry. International finance capital began arriving concomitantly there onwards.

In an empirical analysis, C.P. Chandrasekhar draws interesting conclusions on changing structural linkages in the Indian economy between 1968-69 and 1993-94, during which demand for a unit industrial output coming from agriculture is reduced from 0.247 to 0.087, it is almost replaced by the service sector from 0.237 to 0.457 (Chandrasekhar 2007, 5–6). This weakening of the industry-agricultural linkage, which declined sharply during the 1990s, suggests the non-agrarian Indian bourgeoisie does not seem to need to press for a solution to the agrarian question in the classical sense; its functionality has been taken over by non-agrarian, mainly foreign, finance and non-agrarian markets. This, in Bernstein's schema, means that the agrarian question of capital has been bypassed.

The overall economic balance between agriculture and other sectors is difficult to gauge. First, there are two opposite developments from the early 1990s onwards. In the immediate post-reform period, the reduced state subsidies to agriculture is somewhat compensated by improvement of its terms of trade (relative prices) (Dev 2009). Second, it is strongly debated whether, state support resulted in a net transfer of value to agriculture or, on the contrary, the surplus was siphoned off from agriculture in the neoliberal period (Jan and Harriss-White 2012). Hence, the combined effects of present-day developments are not known fully. However, it remains undeniable that the overall tendency of weakening of the links between agriculture and the rest of the economy has firmly taken place.

Actual Developments

Neoliberalism, Agricultural Transformation and Crisis in India

A careful reading of evidence points to a more complex picture of the agrarian scenario in India than the picture of untrammelled crisis, described by the Left parties and academics like Utsa Patnaik. It is difficult to claim a growth crisis in agriculture in the neoliberal period. In fact the Planning Commission estimates show that the agricultural growth rate during 1991-96 was 4.9 per cent, which fell to 0.5 per cent during 1997-02, but recovered to 2.9 per cent for the period 2003-9. The capital formation is also observed to have continuously increased during this period.[7] In addition, there are clear regional variations. According to the estimates of G.S. Bhalla and Gurmail Singh (2009) for 1990–3 to 2003–6, 6 out of 17 states had agricultural growth rates of above 2 per cent per annum, while three experienced negative growth.[8] Even though states that performed high growth in the earlier phase are facing environmental degradation, salinity of soil and increasing soil erosion (Reddy and Mishra 2009), it is still profitable to continue 'soil mining' in the short run.

However, there are issues to worry about with respect to the structure and nature of the capitalist growth. The overall character of agriculture is steadily changing. Since the early 1980s, the agriculture dependent workforce has declined from 67 per cent to 49 per cent. How welcome is this change? The change in the occupation structure is not conforming to the classical transition in the sense, there is no change in relative labour absorption in the manufacturing sector; instead, only the construction and service sector have expanded. Manufacturing employment is stuck round 11 per cent of total employment since the early 1980s. GDP growth, likewise, is led by the service sector, instead of manufacturing, which makes growth highly unequal and unsustainable.

Agrarian Classes: Landlords and Rich Capitalist Farmers

The question is, then, which social groups are spearheading this growth trajectory? Before investigating the evidence, the conceptual frame should be established. Bernstein's classical definition of peasants as petty commodity producers combining the role of capital and labour within the household is an acceptable starting point.

Patnaik's labour exploitation is useful to classify the peasants as net labouring households or net farming households, which are linked to capital accumulation. On top of the pyramid is the class of big capitalist farmers and capitalist landlords who, while accumulating through the exploitation of labour, do not participate in agricultural work themselves, at most, they engage in farm management activities. They will only invest in agriculture if this is more profitable than to sharecrop out the land and invest in other activities (Patnaik 1986, 1987; Ramachandran 2011).

Contrary to the CPM's position of predominant existence of ex-landlords as large farmers, there has been a significant rise in middle-caste small/middle farmers farmers, other than belonging to the ex-landlord caste/class across India, groups such as the Jats and Yadavs in northern India and the Vokkaligas in Karnataka, Reddy-Kamma-Kapu-OBCs in Andhra Pradesh. While in some parts, rich peasants that drove the capitalist transformation as in case of Punjab, in the rest of India it is the petty commodity producers who did the job, not ex-landlords (Byres 1991, 64). Agriculture has extended dominantly to two seasons, Kharif as well as Rabi, thanks to rural electrification, proliferation of tubewells and diversification of dryland farming into non-food crops (Reddy and Mishra 2009). This said, village-based ex-landlords could be important in UP, Bihar and other parts, their description as dominant section, even there, seem not to hold any more.[9] Scores of village level studies have indicated the sharp decline of power and presence of ex-landlords in the countryside, transition of them into capitalist farmers, and no major difference between rich farmers and them (Ramachandran et al. 2010; Rakshit 2011; Ramachandran 2011; Rao and Reddy 2008)[10] Both groups dominate village life economically and politically; both groups seek access to state power and the corruption money that flows from that; and both groups tend to engage in economic activities outside agriculture, agricultural trade and moneylending (Ramachandran et al. 2010, 86; Ramachandran

2011, 58–60: see also Pattenden 2011). However, the CPM in its 2008 political resolution does not mention landlordism (CPI(M) 2008), which may mean a lesser focus on landlordism. Taking a different direction, Patnaik, on the other hand, now argues that landlord capitalists have reverted to 'extracting through land rent and usurious interests' (Patnaik 2006)–that is, have reverted to semi-feudal activities–but she does not provide additional evidence in support of this.

Official statistics provides no clues on any systematic behaviour across size-wise holdings with respect to investment, accumulation and labour exploitation[11]. This means that case study material is an analytically better source even though, of course, it is very limited in its coverage.

The evidence from both the village studies bring out more nuanced insights. Studies by Ramachandran (2010) and Rakshit (2011) suggests that the capitalist farmers who manage their own farms, being net buyers of wage labour are the most productive. Second, the most productive and high income class in the villages is that of big capitalist farmers/landlords, who manage their farms by hiring wage labour or fully leasing out their farms. (Ramachandran et al. 2010, 92; Rakshit 2011). There does appear to be a considerable variation in this pattern. However, case studies indicate even small farmers occasionally do well. In states such as West Bengal, which have a very high proportion of small and marginal farmers are no less important, commanding 86 per cent of the total agricultural output. In Punjab, by comparison, the figure is only 19 per cent and the all-India average is 51 per cent. Overall, the case studies support the view that not only do both big capitalist farmers and ex-landlords play an important role in the capitalist development in Indian agriculture, but so do capitalist farmers who participate in the work themselves. So do, at least in some parts of India, the peasant petty commodity producers. Even if one considers the landlords' character as 'feudal', who practise tenancy, according to NSSO data, in 2002–3, their share is only 6.5 per cent of operated area was under tenancy (NCEUS 2008, 56). Middle farmers are observed to invest more in mechanization than the large farmers, even though there is a positive relation between farm size and modern farm inputs (NSSO 2003). Input surveys on the other hand have conveyed contrary relations, the farm size perhaps do not match well with social class.

Even though the sharecropping contracts do not necessarily involve pre-capitalist relations, but rational risk sharing practices, which can be no less dynamic in adopting better farm management practices, sharecropping is somehow associated with backwardness. Even if we accept the premise that it involves traditional feudal relations, such systems appear to exist in specific states and regions within those states (Basole and Basu 2011). The pattern seems to be that within generally less agriculturally developed states, the big landowners are not investing in highly productive agriculture, such as in eastern and north eastern states. Even within developed states, backward regions/villages have sharecropping.

Agrarian Classes: The Poor Peasant–'Large Peasant' Spectrum

We shall now move on to the remaining agrarian classes–the huge majority of the rural population. Conceptually, Bernstein suggests that capital today is so dominant that it shapes social class relations in a very direct way, not necessarily in the dominant capital-labour relation. Instead it operates through social classes of self-employed, whose labour is exploited indirectly. This constitutes the so-called informal sector. (Bernstein 2008, 18).

This self-employed class of labour own some means of production, but uses its own labour. Competitive conditions deny not only profits, but even value to their labour. The identity of these, indeed, may alternate between that of wage worker and small-scale petty commodity producer. In agriculture, they could manifest as net food buyers. Marginal and small farmers in agriculture, typically constitute this category. About 42 per cent of rural households constitute landless households (Rawal 2008). Together, the social classes of labour that Bernstein outlines can constitute well over 80 per cent of rural households, who are directly and indirectly exploited.

In the neoliberal era, a large proportion of cultivators were adversely hit by the 1997–2003 agricultural crisis. NSSO data shows that in 2003 the average income for farmers operating less than 4 hectares as negative (NCEUS 2008, 59). This also indicates that even highly productive petty commodity producers could have been losing out, something the Andhra Pradesh case study also documented. The West Bengal case study shows that after liberalization and the entry of MNCs into the trade squeezed out at least some landlord/big capitalist farmers (Rakshit 2011). However, the social group worst hit appears to be the group of petty commodity producers aiming to become proper capitalist farmers through (usurious) loan-based investments in high-value cash crops, and who were caught out when prices crashed from 1997 onwards. It was primarily from within this group that the victims of the 'suicide wave' of the late 1990s and early 2000s came (Reddy and Mishra 2009).

To quickly wrap up, given the general trend that the agrarian system is skewed against the poorer cultivators who suffer lower profitability due to higher costs of production, lower access to technology and formal markets, the long-term growth seems to be sustained by various factors. There are occasional price spikes that pass the incremental benefits to the farm sector. Even though diminished in levels, state support continues to matter, in terms of procurement, irrigation, subsidized fertilizers, subsidized farm equipment and farm loan waivers. This is what has sustained the agriculture, despite liberalization, exposure to MNCs and agribusiness, and environmental degradation. Major regional differences in investment in agriculture and in productivity continue. The spread and intensification of capitalist agriculture appears to be driven by capitalist farmers who also partake in the production themselves, as well as by the class of (ex)landlords and big capitalist farmers, whose involvement in production is limited to a managerial role at most. Petty commodity producers also play a role in the dynamic agricultural regions. Neither for the present period nor for the 1997–2003 crisis, is there much evidence that big capitalist farmers/capitalist landlords chose to revert to pre-capitalist production relations.

While the average farm size continues to fall, there is no hard evidence of large-scale concentration of land, an aspect of peasant differentiation, driving out the small farmers. Case studies point to a steady export of profits by the big and middle farmers and as ex-landlords to exploit urban opportunities. It is unlikely that all agricultural classes are experiencing pauperization, at least a narrow class, diversified its investments in more profitable areas like seed production, orchards, livestock and poultry, floriculture, aqua-culture, and fisheries, integrated with agribusiness with deep pockets, is benefiting economically in a substantial way.

The Labouring Poor, Social Security and Land

As already mentioned, NSSO data shows that in 2002–3 the average marginal and small farmer household had a negative income and often survived on credit. Poverty increased with smaller size of landholding and also down the caste ladder (NCEUS 2008, 12–13). The capitalist development in agriculture clearly did not benefit the poor majority of cultivators. These 'labouring classes' experienced a continued marginalization within agriculture and are compelled to seek employment even outside agriculture–where types of work on offer and remuneration also are regulated by the caste/ethnicity hierarchy, in broad terms.

The large class of 40 per cent landless households, with no homesteads, are principally wage earners. For even small/marginal farmers, who are net buyers of food amongst the labouring classes, are not the same with regard to food prices/agricultural produce prices. Landless labourers, as well as small cultivators who are net food buyers, are becoming de-linked from agriculture for a growing dependence on non-farm employment, therefore, their well-being may well be linked to low agricultural prices, which benefit the non-farm sector. They may look for more direct welfare transfer from the state, like the public distribution system, and other programmes, rather than higher farm gate prices. Welfare programme implementation may be varied across states, thereby keeping the conditions of labouring classes varied.

For labouring classes, a range of welfare policies can be manded by the Left, including land redistribution. as Rawal estimated that 15 million acres surplus land is still available, if ceiling laws are strictly implemented. Even if such surplus land is uniformly distributed, which is highly unlikely, when this is distributed among the landless, the average land available for distribution is only 0.35 acres to each of the 57.6 million landless households (Rawal 2009). Since, land takeover from ex-landlords is unlikely to have any adverse effects, as they do not reinvest in land augmentation, this land reform, in spite of being unproductive or inefficient (as Byres holds), but still may serve the subsistence reform in the agrarian question of labour, in the Bernstein sense.

Expropriation of land from whosoever surfeit landowners, in Rawal's estimates, lessens the focus on ex-landlords, getting away from strict class analysis in any case. Politcally, even Gandhians supported distribution of homestead lands. But eventually in practice, after a long procrastination, only a few states came forward to implement it and even those lands given and going to be given belong to very poor quality (National Coucil for Land Reforms 2009 Report).

It is doubtful for such a limited land distribution programme, an effective class struggle can actually be mustered. Within the land question, a consolation that can be considered is the new compensation criteria in the new Land Acquisition Act 2013, which provides a framework for better compensation for landowners losing land to infrastructural, industrial and mining projects, as well as for other groups losing out in the process. This is a reaction to the increasing struggle of the petty commodity producers against land appropriation.

A land reform to improve the conditions of the landless is only last in the mainstream political agenda. Another area, where it is difficult to point out a success is the struggle against displacement of people, particularly most vulnerable groups like Adivasis (tribals), in mining, hydroelectrical projects and SEZs. Activists succeeded in making the state extend the limited social security, while waging a losing battle to save the land. These struggles are not the typical class struggles, but nevertheless, impinge on livelihoods of people.

The rural employment guarantee programme (MNGREGA) is a notable success that perhaps the left has achieved through lobbying well with the ruling party. Despite opposition to it in many states, from big farmers, the limited implementation had palpable effects in terms of raising the bargaining power of labour and rise in wages (Chandrasekhar and Ghosh 2011).

Conclusion

India is not experiencing a classical agrarian transition. Neoliberal globalization has effectively trumped the previous home market-orientated development model in India, including the relatively slow ongoing agrarian transition. Today, agriculture does not appear to significantly support growth in Indian non-agricultural sectors, neither through capital transfers nor through the creation of a major rural market for industrial produce. That said, surplus value created in agriculture does feed into accumulation of traders-cum-moneylenders, agro-industries and multinational companies operating in the up- and downstream agriculturally related industries, and the specific effects of this are yet to be investigated. In spite of the absence of a substantive classical agrarian transition, the doomsday scenario of Patnaik and McMichael's 'corporate food regime' has not materialized. Neither has a general pauperization of all agrarian classes taken place, not even during the 1997–2003 crisis. Instead, the indications are that the classical processes of peasant differentiation, despite being weak, may well still be ongoing.

Indian agriculture continued to exhibit a rise in capital formation and moderately high growth. Such growth seems to have been achieved in spite of neoliberal reforms which are not supportive of the farm sector. There has been a substantial proliferation and diversification of production into dry land cultivation and high value production. There are no signs of overall farm distress, while petty commodity producers appear to be badly affected during slumps. The decreased average size of the holdings of the majority does support the subsistence of the labouring classes. Most of them earn a substantial income from non-farm wage activitity. Therefore, social security becomes the political demand, which is served by the public distribution system, employment guarantee, rural pensions, etc.

Land reforms, as a means of transferring land to more efficient producers ceased to be relavant. However, it can be still relevant for serving the cause of equity and livelihood. However, the prospects of finding surplus lands, though exists in principle, appear to be remote given the opposition and resistance of the establishment. Nor is the capital interested to back them up for faster capitalist development, as stated above. Under such altered conditions, it is antithetical for left parties to maintain land reforms as their major programme and the principal contradiction is with feudalism. It would be difficult to draw class alliances for such a goal, where their interests are not shared widely. This possibly explains the divergence between this conceptual stand and actual party programme engaged more in lobbying for social security.

Probably there are deep-rooted problems in considering neoliberal globalization as detrimental to all agrarian classes. Ideas of 'people's democracy' in left parties in India are based on the presumption to restore the political economy to pre-neoliberal times, re-establish national industrial policy, its linkages between with agriculture, by way of a return to a classical model of agrarian transition. This is not clear how they are going to muster a broad alliance for such a shift. How do they coax the classes that participate and thrive in the neoliberal division of labour, its modes of labour exploitation and accumulation, complicated by the discursive nature of the labouring classes, which are already divided by the pre-existing factors? Both types of divide are mediated, as always in India, by caste, ethnicity, and gender. Across the board, ruthless exploitation of the labouring classes, as highlighted by so many studies, is the order of the day in India. It is hard to envisage the labour-exploiting classes abandoning their relatively cosy relationship to international neoliberalism and opting for an alliance with the labouring poor, which would inevitably challenge the existing order.

NOTES

1. This is a short version of the orginal paper titled 'The Agrarian Question in Neoliberal India: Agrarian Transition Bypassed?' *Journal of Agrarian Change*, Vol. 13, No. 3, July 2013, pp. 382-404. Jens Lerche, Department of Development Studies, SOAS, University of London, Thornhaugh Street, Russell Square, London WC1H 0XG, UK. E-mail: jl2@soas.ac.uk.
2. See also Bernstein (1994) for a systematic discussion.
3. In fact, the correlation between productivity and agrarian classes defined by the extent to which they hire in/hire out labour is stronger than the correlation between farm size and productivity (Rakshit 2011).
4. The first of these challenges to the classical position has its political and organizational expression in groups such as Via Campesina, GRAIN and the Food Sovereignty movement.
5. Haroon Akram-Lodhi and Cristobel Kay list six agrarian questions that are different from the classical one. Analytically, however, in my view only two of these challenge the classical agrarian question; the four others included in their list deal with issues of a different order.
6. Economic holding refers to the necessary size holding that can generate a profit for the farmer on the full cost of production.
7. Among other things, the paper showed that while public investment in agriculture fell throughout the first decade of liberalization, including during the crisis years, such investments have been increasing again, slowly, since 2002 (Ramachandran 2011, 55-6, 73-5).
8. The + 2 per cent growth states were Gujarat (5.33 per cent); Rajasthan (3.21 per cent), Madhya Pradesh (including Chhattisgarh) (2.52 per cent), West Bengal (2.39 per cent), Haryana (2.30 per cent) and Maharashtra (2.13 per cent), while the negative growth states were Odisha (-0.67 per cent), Kerala (-0.80 per cent) and Tamil Nadu (-1.46 per cent) (Bhalla and Singh 2009, 35). The state categories used are the 'old' states as they were organized in the 1990s. In the north-east, Assam is the exception to this rule.
9. The NSSO figures indicate that landownership of medium and large farmers may have fallen fairly constantly since 1953-4 but

by 2003-4, the 7 per cent of the landowners who operated more than 4 hectares were still in charge of 34 per cent of the land (NCEUS 2008, 4). However, while NSSO data in general is reliable, underreporting by large landowners is commonplace, due to the Indian land ceiling legislation, so it may well be that the numbers and land sizes of large-scale landowners are significantly higher.

10. That said, Ramachandran appears in places to maintain that ex-landlords and rich farmers are usefully dealt with as two different sub-categories within an overall joint category (Ramachandran 2011, 58–9).
11. Apart from marginal farmers who are unlikely to be labour exploiting but who can, nevertheless, be engaged in capital accumulating production processes.

REFERENCES

Akram-Lodhi, H. and C. Kay, 2010. 'Surveying the Agrarian Question (Part 2): Current Debates and Beyond', *Journal of Peasant Studies*, 37 (2): 255–84.

Bernstein, H., 1994. 'Agrarian Classes in Capitalist Development'. In *Capitalism and Development*, ed. L. Sklair, 40–71. London: Routledge.

Bernstein, H., 1996. 'Agrarian Questions: Then and Now', *Journal of Peasant Studies*, 24 (1–2): 22–59.

Bernstein, H., 2006. 'Is There an Agrarian Question in the 21st Century?' *Canadian Journal of Development Studies*, 27 (4): 449–60.

Bernstein, H., 2008. 'Agrarian Change in a Globalising World: (Final) Farewells to the Peasantry?' Paper Presented at the *Journal of Agrarian Change* Workshop, SOAS, 1–2 May.

Bernstein, H., ed., 2010. 'Productive Forces in Capitalist Agriculture: Political Economy and Political Ecology', Special Issue, *Journal of Agrarian Change*, 10 (3).

Bhalla, G.S. and G. Singh, 2009. 'Economic Liberalisation and Indian Agriculture : A Statewise Analysis', *Economic and Political Weekly*, 44 (52): 34–44.

Byres, T.J., 1986. 'The Agrarian Question and Differentiation of the Peasantry'. Introduction to A. Rahman, *Peasants and Classes : A Study of Differentiation in Bangladesh*. London: Zed Books.

Byres, T.J., 1991. 'The Agrarian Question and Differing Form of Capitalist Agrarian Transition: An Essay with Reference to Asia'. In *Rural Transformation in Asia*, eds J. Breman and S. Mundle, 3-76. New Delhi: Oxford University Press.

Byres, T.J., 1995. 'Political Economy, Agrarian Question and Comparative Method', *Economic and Political Weekly*, 30 (10): 507-13.

Byres, T.J., 1996. *Capitalism from Above and Capitalism from Below : An Essay in Comparative Political Economy*. Basingstoke: Macmillan.

Byres, T.J., 2003. 'Structural Change, the Agrarian Question and the Possible Impact of Globalization'. In *Work and Well-Being in the Age of Finance*, eds. J. Ghosh and C.P. Chandrasekhar, 171-211. New Delhi: Tulika Books.

Byres, T.J., 2009. 'The Landlord Class, Peasant Differentiation, Class Struggle and the Transition to Capitalism: England, France and Prussia Compared', *Journal of Peasant Studies*, 36 (1): 33-54.

Chand, R., P.A. Lakshmi Prasanna and A. Singh, 2011. 'Farm Size and Productivity: Understanding the Strengths of Smallholders and Improving Their Livelihoods', *Economic and Political Weekly*, 46 (26-7): 5-11.

Chandrasekhar, C.P. and J. Ghosh, 2010. Controlling Food Prices. Macroscan, http://www.macroscan.org (accessed July 7, 2011).

CPI(M) (Communist Party of India (Marxist)), 2008. Political Resolution Adopted at the Congress of the Communist Party of India (Marxist) March 29 to April 3, 2008, Coimbatore, http://cpim.org/documents/19%20per%20cent20 Congress.Political.Resolution.pdf (accessed July 7, 2011).

CPI(M) (Communist Party of India (Marxist), n.d. Communist Party of India (Marxist) website, http://cpim.org/ (accessed July 7, 2011).

CPI(Maoist) (Communist Party of India (Maoist)), 2004. Party Programme. Central Committee (P), http:// www.bannedthought.net/India/CPI-Maoist-Docs/Founding/Programme-pamphlet.pdf (accessed July 7, 2011).

CPI(ML) (Communist Party of India (Marxist-Leninist)), 2007. Agrarian Programme, http://www.cpiml.org/ 8th_congress/cpiml_agrarian_programme.html (accessed 7 July 2011).

Deb, S., 2002. 'The Debate on Agriculture-Industry Terms of Trade in India'. Working Paper No. 109, Centre for Development

Economics, Department of Economics, Delhi School of Economics, http://www.cdedse.org (accessed February 22, 2013).

Deshpande, R.S., 2008. 'Price Policy and Minimum Support Prices in a Changing Agricultural Economy'. In *Reforming Indian Agriculture. Towards Employment Generation and Poverty Reduction*, ed. S.K. Bhaumik, 119–60. New Delhi: Sage Publications.

Dev, S.M., 2009. 'Structural Reforms and Agriculture: Issues and Policies'. Keynote Paper on Agriculture 92nd Annual Conference of the Indian Economic Association, December 27–29, http://cacp.dacnet.nic.in/ Structural_Reforms_and_Agriculture.pdf (accessed February 22, 2013).

Dyer, G., 2004. 'Redistributive Land Reform: No April Rose. The Poverty of Berry and Cline and GKI on the Inverse Relationship', *Journal of Agrarian Change*, 4 (1&2): 45–72.

Harriss, J., J. Jeyaranjan and K. Nagaraj, 2010. 'Land, Labour and Caste Politics in Rural Tamil Nadu in the 20th Century: Iruvelpattu (1916–2008)', *Economic and Political Weekly*, 45 (31): 47–61.

Harriss-White, B., 2008. *Rural Commercial Capital: Agricultural Markets in West Bengal*. New Delhi: Oxford University Press.

Jan, M.A. and B. Harriss-White, 2012. 'The Three Roles of Agricultural Markets: A Review of Ideas about Agricultural Commodity Markets in India', *Economic and Political Weekly*, 47 (52): 39–52.

National Land Reforms Council, http://articles.economictimes.indiatimes.com/2012-06-21/ news/32352262_1_national-land-reforms-council-land-policy-land-acquisition-bill (accessed 1 December 2012).

McMichael, P., 2010. 'The World Food Crisis in Historical Perspective'. In *Agriculture and Food in Crisis. Conflict, Resistance, and Renewal*, eds. F. Magdoff and B. Tokar, 51–68. New York: Monthly Review Press.

Ministry of Agriculture, Government of India, Various Years. *Agricultural Statistics at a Glance*. Department of Agriculture and Cooperation, http://agricoop.nic.in/Agristatistics.htm (accessed July 7, 2011).

NCEUS (National Commission for Enterprises in the Unorganised Sector), 2008. A Special Programme for Marginal and Small Farmers. New Delhi: NCEUS, Government of India, www.nceus.gov.in (accessed July 7, 2011).

Patnaik, U., 1972. 'Development of Capitalism in Agriculture - II', *Social Scientist*, October, 1 (3): 3-19.

Patnaik, U., 1986. 'The Agrarian Question and Development of Capitalism in India', *Economic and Political Weekly*, 21 (18): 781-93.

Patnaik, U., 1987. *Peasant Class Differentiation. A Study in Method with Reference to Haryana*. New Delhi: Oxford University Press.

Patnaik, U., 2006. 'The Agrarian Crisis and Importance of Peasant Resistance', *People's Democracy*, 30 (5), http:// pd.cpim.org/2006/0129/01292006_utsa.htm (accessed 7 July 2011).

Patnaik, U., 2010. The New Primitive Accumulation and the Peasantry. Abstract of P. Sundarayya Memorial Lecture, 19 May 2010, Hyderabad, http://indiacurrentaffairs.org/the-new-primitive-accumulation-and-the-peasantry-utsapatnaik/ (accessed July 7, 2011).

Pattenden, J., 2011. 'Gatekeeping as Accumulation and Domination: Decentralisation and Class Relations in Rural South India', *Journal of Agrarian Change*, 11 (2): 164-94.

Rakshit, S., 2011. 'Capital Intensification, Productivity and Exchange: A Class Based Analysis of Agriculture in West Bengal in the Current Millennium', *Journal of Agrarian Change*, 11 (4): 505-35.

Ramachandran, V.K., V. Rawal and M. Swaminathan, eds., 2010. *Socio-Economic Surveys of Three Villages in Andhra Pradesh: A Study of Agrarian Relations*. New Delhi: Tulika Books.

Rawal, V., 2008. 'Ownership Holdings of Land in Rural India: Putting the Record Straight', *Economic and Political Weekly*, 43 (10): 43-7.

Reddy, D.N. and S. Mishra, 2009. 'Agriculture in the Reforms Regime'. In *Agrarian Crisis in India*, eds. D.N. Reddy and S. Mishra, 3-43. New Delhi: Oxford University Press.

Thorner, A., 1982. 'Semi-Feudalism or Capitalism? Contemporary Debate on Classes and Modes of Production in India', Parts 1, 2 and 3, *Economic and Political Weekly*, 17 (49, 50, 51): 1961-8, 1993-9, 2061-86.

14

Agrarian Conditions in Telangana and AP: Summary of Observations

[R.V. Ramana Murthy]

The states of Telangana and Andhra Pradesh, existing as one state Andhra Pradesh during 1956-2014, in spite of its uneven nature, underwent considerable transformation in the six decades. There are several micro level studies in the literature like Carole Upadhyay (1988), Niranjan Rao and D. Narasimha Reddy (2008), V.K. Ramachandran, Madhura Swaminathan and Vikas Rawal (2009) and S.R. Vidyasagar (2013) that have brought out evidence of changing agrarian conditions of production in rural Andhra Pradesh. There is a growing consensus over the fact that relations of production in the state are evidently capitalist. Some studies are explicit in this conclusion and others implicit. Given the paucity of macro data on crucial aspects of agrarian conditions, there is however, a need for many more studies to confirm certain major trends and this study contributes in this direction. We have seen Basole and Basu (2011) have come up with some important observations over agrarian structure, tenancy, credit, capital formation, wage labour, etc. to examine the dominant mode of surplus accumulation. The authors concluded that compared to five decades ago, the dominant mode of surplus extraction is production for profit exploiting wage labour. The paper presents the summary of field observations undertaken to examine the production conditions and relations, with an additional objective of understanding how rural households cope with the distress and level of income generation across size classes. The field work was undertaken in the year 2013 (the study is published in 2015), by interviewing 1087 households in seven villages in erstwhile combined Andhra Pradesh. Seven villages are drawn from three regions, namely, Telangana, Coastal Andhra, and Rayalaseema. Information is collected over size of holdings, production, costs, investments, returns, prices, non-farm activities, employment, and welfare benefits received. I shall summarize the major findings of the study in the following.

Regarding land ownership, the study finds that the number of households with some access to land is about 95 per cent. If one considers sub-marginal households (owning less than 0.4 acres), the effective landless households is about 25 per cent in the sample villages. Among 75 per cent landed households, 46 per cent are marginal farmers, 20 per cent are small farmers, 19 per cent semi-medium farmers, 13 per cent are medium farmers and 2 per cent are large farmers, following the NSS classification. Among these effectively, 85 per cent farmers are *petty commodity producers* (defined as those who own relatively smaller parcels of land and depend on family labour for farming also hire out as wage labour for farm as well as non-farm activities). Thus even these appear as land owners, but in substantive terms they are workers. The remaining 15 per cent landed households, constituted by medium farmers owning 10-20 acres and large farmers owning more than 20 acres of land, are clearly capitalist farmers, who have the capacity to earn profits in farming by exploiting wage labour. Such classification expects a process of class differentiation as well. Thus as witnessed at national level, the micro data too suggests an expanded Kautskian predicament of large petty commodity producers looming large in agriculture.

Holdings in agriculture are becoming fragmented from above. Small holdings emerge from below and from above. Some previously landless labourers purchased land, as happened until two decades ago. Holdings from above are getting fragmented through property mutation. These two processes are making an increasing number of marginal, small and semi-medium farmers. The share of medium farmers share declined moderately and that of large farmers declined drastically over time. Medium and large households are selling part of their holdings, and leasing out the rest or growing orchards.

Landlessness is generally higher in Coastal Andhra villages (particularly in canal-irrigated ones), in Telangana and Rayalaseema villages it is less. All villages that have dry land or well irrigation, have a lower share of landless labour and are increasingly dependent on mechanization.

An upcoming dominant feature in these villages is the phenomenon of rising tenancy, that began to be seen in different states of India in the past one decade. Tenancy is dominant in villages which have assured irrigation. Small, marginal and landless households are leasing–in land in the tenancy market on fixed rent. Cash rents exist where cash crops are grown and kind rent is preferred in paddy-growing villages. Non-cultivating households in villages are on the rise, who own land that they lease out, who diversify into other activities. Sharecropping is observed only in one village whose irrigation sources are fully rainfall dependent. In contrast to the Basole-Basu study, which observes data only till 2003, this study notes a rising trend of tenancy. But I confirm their view, this tenancy is capitalist in nature.

It is observed that production is essentially for the market. Except for small and marginal farmers who keep a third of the produce for home consumption while selling the rest in the market, all other categories of farmers sell 90 per cent of their produce. Those who produce cash crops sell the entire crop. Thus, general commodity production, a necessary condition for capitalist relations of production, is the dominant feature. Even the petty producers who constitute 85 percent in number, command 65 per cent of total production, contribute a surplus of 75 per cent production to the market. This suggests that production has become predominantly general commodity production, a certain characteristic of capitalist transition.

There has been a significant crop diversification in the past two decades and a shift in the area from food crops to non-foodgrain crops. The traditional crops have disappeared totally. I have observed that peasants aim for self-sufficiency with respect to family needs, and also strive to produce for the market to earn cash revenues.

Substantial investments in pump sets, tractors, rotovators, sprayers, sprinklers, and borewells are made by almost all classes of farmers. Tractors and harvesters are available on lease in all villages. Thus operations are getting mechanized, except weeding, especially in non-foodgrain crops. Knowledge systems of agricultural production remain informal and unprofessional among petty producers, while medium and big farmers are much more professional. Capital formation on average ranged up to about Rs. 1.5 lakhs per acre. Farmers have regular access to commercial banks with an average crop loan of Rs. 15,000 per season and they also raise loans from private moneylenders for production as well as consumption purposes. The credit share of banks of farmers in general is about 52 per cent. Institutional credit has a size bias. However, petty producers are now provided 25 per cent of their credit through women SHGs. The tenant farmers are not covered by the institutional credit, and are forced to rely on private lenders. While instrumental rationality of the farming class even in the lower order appear to be well attained, but reproduction of social relations has become more expensive.

Canal-irrigated areas enjoy subsidized irrigation. Dry land farmers had to make a greater share of private investment, while the state has provided rural electrification. The average use of fertilizers is about 256 kilos per acre. All inputs, including seeds are purchased from the market. It is about two and more decades where relations of production turned dominantly capitalist.

There is a considerable capital investment on pumpsets, tractors, rotovarots, weeders, sprayers, pesticides, fertilizers, sprinklers and micro-irrigation. Harvesters, tractors and other mechanical tools are available in lease market for every size class farmer, which are widely used. The rational response to cost escalation is visible in adoption of mechanization.

The field observations revealed that the medium and big farmers enjoy higher yields, lower costs and greater profitability. This is found to be the case for most crops such as paddy, maize, cotton, turmeric, and sugarcane.

The study found that average profitability for 9 crops is positive only over simple paid-out costs (without considering rent on own land, interest on fixed cost and family labour) of owner-cultivators. But once family labour and rent paid is accounted profitability became marginal or zero for most crops except for turmeric, which is a high value commodity. When rent on own land, interest on fixed capital and 10 per cent margin profit is considered, the gross profit would became negative. However, profitability is marginally better for medium and large farmers. The average annual return per acre for paddy is found to be Rs. 12,000 per annum, Rs. 10,000 for cotton, Rs. 9,000 for maize over paid out cost+family labour. The profitability tends to be below the market rent, which makes leasing, if available, a rational option. Thus the present conditions appear to give extremely poor returns to the farmers. Farming has lost the ability to sustain the farmers. Petty producers, who supplement their incomes with wage income and use family labour to a considerable extent, appear to carry the agricultural sector. The study found that agriculture supports only 45-55 per cent of household income in villages. The rest of the income is earned from non-farm activities. However, this static picture apart, occasional windfall profits also sustain the optimism of the peasants, which wears off gradually. Intense competition among the farmers does not appear to allow any long-term gains, market prices tend to eliminate any profitability, keeping the peasantry earning a bare subsistence.

The returns of sugarcane over paid out costs as well as full costs are positive for small farmers and large, while negative for marginal, semi-medium and medium farmers. The sugarcane cultivation gives about Rs. 25,000 average return over full cost with an average 20 tonne yield.

Tobacco, with a yield of about 5-9 quintals, returns about Rs. 22,500 net per acre for a medium and semi-medium farmer;

Rs. 3,500-7,500 for marginal and small farmer over paid out costs. Returns fall to Rs. 6,000-9,000 per acre over full cost. Turmeric, cultivated in selected pockets, brings handsome returns of Rs. 54,000-68,000 per acre. Thus regional and class differences exist in accumulation.

On average in poor agricultural households, men work from 21 to 10 days on their own farms, depending on size class. Women work about 42 to 19 days per annum on their own farms. Aggregate employment (on own farm and hiring themselves out) decreases over size class. Petty producers also hire in labour during the peak operations. Finally, they hire themselves out as wage labour. Average wage employment is 73 days for men and 103 days for women. Aggregate (own farm + hired out) employment on average is less than 100 days for men and 150 days for women. Attached labour (on an annual contract) is very expensive and seldom exists. This indicates two things, first increased feminization of agricultural employment and second, low employment availability, as suggested by several studies. Mahatma Gandhi National Rural Employment Guarantee Scheme in the study villages reportedly provided 45-80 days of employment. MGNREGA employment is sought by small peasants as well as landless labour. The crisis of unemployment is always round the corner.

The average wage rate for a male in agriculture in normal times is Rs. 220-250; Rs. 175-225 for female labour. Peak wage is in a range of Rs. 300-350 for male labour and Rs. 200-300 for female labour. We see a trend of rising wage rate on one hand and declining employment availability on the other, probably the latter is a response to the former through mechanization.

The average rural family business income ranges between from Rs. 1,07,222 for marginal-semi medium farm households and Rs. 3,00,000 for medium-large farm households. Thus a definite process of class differentiation is also in place. More importantly, there is a considerable diversification of income from farm to non-farm activities among rural households. Roughly, 45 per cent of income is derived from non-farm activities. While, the family income of marginal-small farm household income appears to be higher than the official poverty line given by the Planning Commission, 75 per cent are still poor under the international norm of $ 2 per day.

Interestingly, most rural households receive welfare transfers from the state. At least six to seven schemes directly transfer welfare benefits in kind and cash to 90 per cent of rural households in the state: for example, the public distribution system, employment guarantee, pensions, scholarships, midday meal, and health insurance. The average transfer to a rural household by a conservative measure is about Rs. 19,000 per annum, and the poorest receive about Rs. 23,000 per annum.

Kalyan Sanyal (2007) and Chatterjee (2009) have argued that the Indian state executes a Polanyian 'double movement', mitigation measures against the poverty of rural households, the liberal democracy over a period is compelled to design efficient welfare transfers. In our observations we have noted several welfare measures, like public distribution, pensions, MGNREGA employment, midday meals, health insurance, microfinance loans, etc., are implemented with reasonable effectiveness in the state. Small differences that may exist between the two states of Telangana and Andhra Pradesh in welfare measures are more due to differences in administrative efficacy. There is no resistance to these from big landlords. The changing agrarian structure and social change has something to do with this. The relations of production are organized entirely through market mechanisms, the nature of these production relations is more obvious than ever before.

Conclusion

The generalized commodity production, wage labour, dominating production for market, crop diversification in attempt to earn cash revenues, gradually growing mechanization, capitalist tenancy markets found by this study, as done by others strongly suggest a definite capitalist transformation. When it comes to the question of increasing small holdings managed by petty commodity producers, low and falling returns, significant indebtedness, occupation diversification by farmers in general and wage income by petty producers suggests trends Kautsky has elaborated in his work. While

19th century capitalism itself did not eliminate the small peasantry in advanced capitalist countries, as Kalyan Sanyal, Bernstein, Akram-Lodhi and Kay suggested, it is impossible to do so in the case of postcolonial 20th century capitalism. The growing capitalist nature of production makes more and more surplus labour in agriculture, with people who exist or undertake temporary migration to urban spaces. This is the condition of capitalism in periphery. The bourgeoisie in India are possibly too aware of this condition, and make welfare transfers to mitigate the survival crisis for the petty producers and the proletariat. This study brings evidence to this effect. Particularly, after the introduction of neoliberal reforms, the farm sector appears to be exposed to naked market forces without an effective safety net intervention for most crops. This is making big and middle level farmers to quit and lease their lands while small and marginal farmers to hang on rather than to join the reserve army. The locus of surplus appropriation has moved out of farming, subjecting it to indirect exploitation of the sectors' labour belonging to petty producers. In my opinion, the existence of small holdings, growing tenancy and agrarian distress are not a sign of crisis imposed by 'semi-feudalism', rather this crisis created by developing capitalist relations, where a *rentier* class that exists in the form of landlords, commission agents, traders, fertilizer and pesticide suppliers and moneylenders, manages to squeeze the surplus from the exchange process, driving their subjects to precarity.

REFERENCES

Akram-Lodhi, Haroon and Christobel Kay (2010). 'Surveying the Agrarian Question' (Part I & II) in *Journal of Peasant Studies*, Vol. 37, No. 1 & 2, April 2010, pp. 177-202 and 255-284.

Bernstein, Henry, 1996. 'Agrarian Questions Now and Then' in Bernstein, Henry and Tom Brass (1996) edited *Agrarian Questions: Essays in Appreciation of T.J. Byres*, Frank Cass, London, pp. 22-59.

Byres, T.J., 1986. 'The Agrarian Question, Forms of Capitalist Transition and the State: An Essay with Reference to Asia' *Social Scientist*, Vol. 3, No. 126.

Chatterjee, Partha, (2008). 'Democracy and Economic Transformation in India', *Economic and Political Weekly*, April 19.

Kautsky, Karl, 1988. *The Agrarian Question*, Zwan Publications, London and Winchester.

Lerche, Jens, 2013. 'The Agrarian Questin in Neolibaral India: Agrarian Transition Bypassed?' in *Journal of Agrarian Change*, Vol. 13, No. 3, July, pp. 382-404.

Marx, Karl, 1954. *Das Capital*, Vol. I, Part III, Progress Publishers, Moscow.

Patnaik, Utsa, 1987. *Peasant Class Differentiation: A Study in Method with Reference to Haryana*, Oxford University Press, New Delhi.

Polyani, Karl, 1944. *The Great Transformation: The Political and Economic Origins of our Times*, Beacon Press, Boston.

Ramachandran, V.K., Vikas Rawal and Madhura Swaminathan 2010. *Socio-Economic Surveys of Three Villages in Andhra Pradesh: A Study of Agrarian Relations*, Tulika, New Delhi.

Ramana Murthy and Rekha Mishra, 2012. *Unremunerative Pricing of Paddy: A Case of Andhra Pradesh*, DRG-RBI study, URL: rbidocs.rbi.org.in/rdocs/Publications/PDFs/ FPP180912FLS.pdf.

Ramana Murthy, 2013a. 'Political Economy of Agrarian Crisis and Subsistence Under Neoliberalism in India' *The NEHU Journal*, Vol. XI, No. 1, January.

Reddy, Narsimha and Sujit Mishra, 2009. edited *Agrarian Crisis in India*, Oxford University Press, New Delhi.

Reddy, D.N. and G.N. Rao, 2008. edited *Rural Transformation: Perspectives from Village Studies in Andhra Pradesh*, Daanish Publications, New Delhi.

Sanyal, Kalyan, 2007. *Rethinking Capitalist Development: Primitive Accumulation, Governmentality, and Post-Colonial Capitalism*, Routledge, London.

Vidyasagar, S.R., 2014. *Unheard Voices*, Gyan Publishers, New Delhi.

Thorner, A., 1982. 'Semi-Feudalism or Capitalism: Contemporary Debate on Classes and Modes of Production in India, *Economic and Political Weekly*, Vol. XVII, No. 51, December 18.

Vijay, R., 2006. "Agrarian Structure and Agrarian Relations: Illustrations from Village Studies" in *Studies in Humanities and Social Sciences*, Vol. 2, No. 1.

Upadhyay, Carol, 1988. 'The Farmer-Capitalists of Coastal Andhra Pradesh', *Economic and Political Weekly*, Vol. 23, No. 28 (July 9, 1988), pp. 1433-1442.

15

Dalits and the Land Question: A View from the Ground

[S.R. Vidyasagar]

Even during the colonial period, Dalits waged several struggles against the social and economic oppression of the caste society. Dr. B.R. Ambedkar played a leading role in these struggles and fought for the cause of Dalits. Consequently, colonial rulers made some corrective steps to improve the condition of Dalits. The post-independent state took several steps of affirmative actions, mostly in education and job opportunities in government jobs. The preamble of the Constitution of India in its directive principles explicitly stated to bring social and economic equality in the country. This should apply to land ownership also. In the entire land reforms acts and land redistribution programme, some land transfer is expected in favour of Dalits or Scheduled Castes as referred. There are 59 officially recognized Scheduled Castes in the state of Andhra Pradesh. They constitute 10.91 per cent of population, roughly the same at the national level. They do not even own 1 per cent of arable land in the state or in India. In this paper, I will present my observations on the efforts of the Indian state in providing land to Dalits, who were deprived of land for ages, even the meagre extent to which it provided what kinds of lands that they were, how caste society thwarted every attempt of Dalits to bring them under cultivation, forced to transfer some of these lands back to themselves. I will also shed some light on the struggle of Dalits to escape the clutches of the obnoxious annual farm servant system in agriculture in their course of migration to urban opportunities. I present these from the field study undertaken in Srikakulam district of Andhra Pradesh state in the period 2005-10.

As Ambedkar rightly observed that proletarians in Indian society existed by social sanction. In his words, "An untouchable must not own and cultivate land and lead an independent life. For his livelihood, he must depend upon stale remnants of food left over by the Hindu households and upon meat of cattle that die in the village. These remnants of food he must collect from door to door. For, he must go on his begging round every evening."

Daniel Thorner, an American political economist, in 1955 also commented in his lectures at Delhi University that "the rare Chamar, Mahar, Panchama or other untouchable who prospects economically and attempts to secure a foothold for his family buying land may find insurmountable obstacles in the way of purchasing" (*The Agrarian Prospect in India*, p. 11, Daniel Thorner). It was hoped that abolition of *Zamindaries* as intermediaries as the major land reform would transfer the land to the actual tiller, it was never recognized that there is another layer of intermediary in the name of 'recorded tenant' who usurped all the land, than the actual tenant who is the real tiller. Thus the Abolition of Intermediaries Act has created the rich peasantry in India. Land that is distributed hardly reached the Dalits, who were the bottom fraction of the tillers. Social and economic oppression continued in society.

Implementation of Land Reforms

In several budget speeches and official documents on land administration, it is stated that the government has the intent to transfer uncultivated lands to Dalits since the 1970s. Amidst several contradictory statistics, we learn that about 24 lakh acres of banjar land, de-reserved forest land were to be distributed to Dalits. However, by the 1980s, no such proclamations are to be found in the budget speeches. During the late 90s, the government declared that the poverty and development of Dalits is linked to education. Hence, focus is shifted from the land to education.

As per state level records, by 1972-73, only about 70,329 acres of land were identified as surplus, there were at least 10.5 lakh Dalit households, on average they could have received 0.33 acres. Subsequently, in 1981-82, a total banjar land to the tune of 5.85 lakh acres had been distributed, among 4.58 lakh beneficiaries. Dalit beneficiaries were 1,88 laks in number, and got land of 2,32 lakh acres, which means an average of 1.23 acres to each. Thus some marginal farmers, by ownership are created by fiat at best (Source: Paper on Land Revenue Administration–A Historical Outlook, C. Umamaheswara Rao, IAS, Commissioner, AMR-APARD).

Further, much of the land distributed is ridden either with legal disputes or unfit for any active cultivation. They neither obtained any institutional loan to improve these lands nor had any sufficient savings from the subsistence wages they earned. Eventually, many have sold their lands to upper castes. An upper-caste individual even triumphantly remarked, "Can the Dalits keep their lands? They are too lazy to do field work." Indeed, the peasantry castes who earned their profits from the surplus labour of Dalits, conveniently forget the source of their own wealth.

In fact, in all the villages I studied, the majority of lands were alienated from Dalits. The land distribution programme thus has worked as indirect means to transfer land to rural rich peasantry. The Agricultural Minister of Andhra Pradesh, Hon'ble Raghuveera Reddy declared: "So far in Andhra Pradesh, the government distributed 46 lakh acres to the landless. Almost 1/10th of the land, i.e. 4.35 lakhs of acres were alienated. Some lands were sold by beneficiaries while some are grabbed. So far, the government had taken over 2.88 lakh acres." (Source: *Andhra Jyothy Daily*, dated January 1, 2013).

Not Even the Endowment Lands

As it is common knowledge that there is substantial land under temple endowment. There were many struggles undertaken by Dalits demanding the state to either lease or transfer to to them.

But even these lands have gone to peasant castes, but not Dalits. I will cite a few examples to show how land transfers took place.

Ajjada in Balijipeta Mandal in Srikakulam district, was traditionally a Brahmin Inamdari village. The Brahmins allegedly a century ago lost a gamble with the zamindar of Bobbili and lost 450 acres in the game. The zamindar refused to take the land, considering it as sacrilege and returned the lands. But the Brahmins refused to till the land. Consequently, the zamindar dedicated those lands to their family God, Venugopalaswamy, and made dominant village peasants as trustees. After the abolition of Inamdaris, they lost economic and social control in the village and the rich peasantry of Koppula Velama caste occupied those lands. Later they did not even pay the nominal rent to the state. They even managed to get ownership over them, started selling and distributing those lands among their kin. In the whole game, they had not considered to distribute even one cent of land to the Dalits of that village.

After prolonged agitations and legal battles, the Dalits of Seebilli Peddavalasa and Kitchada villages could get some of these lands. The expert committee of the Planning Commission recommended 22 years ago, "*Where lands with religious and charitable institutions are leased out, at least, 50 per cent should be earmarked for Scheduled Caste agricultural labour on mutually fair terms.*" *(Quoted in National S.C. Commission Report 1994-95).* The Finance Minister of Andhra Pradesh in 1971-72 budget speech told "*Certain other measures such as leasing out of lands of various institutions to the landless poor on a preferential basis.....*" *(Source: Andhra Pradesh Budget Speech 1971-72).* However, neither the recommendation nor the implementation saw the light in this district.

As per the Endowment Department, in Srikakulam district, endowment lands constitute about 22,649.56 acres and 190 shops. At present, only 11,201 acres remained on paper and 116 Dalit families were tilling less than 250 acres. The official explanation is Dalits could never remit the deposit money to participate in the auction process. Thus Dalits neither got a share in lands illegally occupied nor legally leased out. According to the Deputy

Commissioner of Endowment in a recent interview to the press observed: "In North Andhra, 55,000 acres of land were under the name of the department and out of these, 8,000 acres were occupied." (*Eenadu*, Srikakulam edition, May 10, 2012). For sure, it is not Dalits who occupied those lands.

Even at the national level, the percentage of Dalit cultivators was decreasing. As per the data of the National Scheduled Commission 2004-05, in the year 1961, the share of cultivators among Dalits which was 37.76 per cent in 1961 slipped to 22.08 per cent in 2001. In the state of Andhra Pradesh, the share of cultivators among Dalits has fallen from 58 per cent to 23 per cent during 1981-2001.

Land and Dalits: Some Instances

The abolition of intermediaries, for Srikakulam meant the land power of three upper castes namely, Kshatriyas, Brahmins and Velamas were replaced by upper peasant castes, namely Koppula Velama, Kalinga and Turpu Kapu. Dalits did not get even an inch of land. In some villages, Dalits got wastelands of 1.3 acres per holding, most of these too were alienated to upper castes. I will illustrate three case studies.

Gopannavalasa is a village in Merakamudidam Mandal where the government distributed 6.76 acres of land to Dalits with Turpu Kapus being the major peasant caste here. Turpu Kapus objected to this assignment on the plea that those were tank-bed. Revenue administration clarified that those were not tank-bed. Turpu Kapus disputed that the land allotted to the Dalits receives the rain water first and it flows to the tanks, hence it is tank bed. Dalits began cultivating the lands. Meanwhile, the Turpu Kapus filed a legal case. While the legal proceedings were on, two Dalit leaders of the village representing the cause were murdered. The assassins got the legal case squashed by the High Court. The Dalits dropped their claims on the land.

Tolapi is a village in Ponduru Mandal where the Kalinga caste was the major peasant caste. Government allotted 0.15 acres each to 39 Dalit families during the mid-70s where the Dalits tried to cultivate the land. Kalinga prevented Dalits from cultivating the land given. In every harvest season, they used to drive their cattle to destroy the crop, until finally, the Dalits stopped their cultivation.

Konuru is a village in Garividi Mandal where Kshatriya families owned almost 90 per cent of the agricultural land. They perpetrated violent dominance in the village, affecting everyone. To escape Ceiling Laws, they surreptitiously registered land in the name of Dalits who were working as labourers in their fields. A Dalit named Majji Tamanna, got to know and protested and demanded the ownership of the land. Turpu Kapus, who were the second dominant peasant caste, who were also victims of this domination of Kshatriyas, expressed their solidarity to Tammanna. Then this pushed the Kshatriyas on the back foot. Slowly, Turpu Kapus began their assertion after their caste leader Sriramulunaidu became the unchallenged leader under TDP rule. Unable to stomach their decline, the Kshatriyas violently attacked the Dalit locality after knowing Majji Tamanna went to administration to restore land registered to Dalits in whose names it was registered. Thanks to an NGO 'Shodhana' which threw its weight behind the Dalits, helped criminal cases registered against the Kshatriyas, put pressure on the district administration to execute the land restoration. Changing political climate in the state also helped to ease the situation. But Dalits for a long time did not dare to till those lands that were given to them. Kunuru stands as a rare example where Dalits eventually got access to small parcels of an extremely violent struggle. Afterwards, Dalits refused to work for Kshatriyas, and decided to migrate. Kshatriyas were forced to plant mango orchards which does not require much labour.

Boddam is a village in Rajam Mandal. Polinati Velama is the major peasant caste here. During the late 70s, the government distributed 40 acres to 60 Dalit families who tried to cultivate the lands. The peasant caste obstructed the cultivation and attacked the Dalits physically. The Dalits lodged a complaint in the police station at Rajam. The complaint was registered because the sub-inspector happened to be a Dalit. Of course, nothing much happened and the lands remained uncultivated for a long time.

Dalaipeta is a village in Komarada Mandal. Despite the best efforts of two Dalit IAS officers, the Dalits could not cultivate in the village. The Dalits occupied the lands under the banner of the then undivided Communist Party of India (CPI) during the early 60s. Actually, this land belonged to the Hill zamindar of Kurupam. The government had not conferred the title to anyone on the land. Since it was rain-fed land, Dalits could not do much remunerative cultivation. During the late 1970s, Shri B. Danam, the then District Collector tried to provide irrigation facilities to the lands by planning to build a reservoir in Madalangi village only to channelize the water from Gummadigedda, a regular stream from the hill tracts. The villagers of Madalangi objected to this plan on the pretext of inundation of the lands of their village. They went to the court and brought a judgment in their favour. Hence, the proposed project was shelved. Again during the early 90s, the then collector Mrs. Shri Radha sanctioned the lift irrigation scheme and the water to be drawn from the river Nagavali. The Dalits had to manage it with collective efforts. For two years with unity, the Dalits managed it well and reaped some benefits. The upper caste peasants divided the community in the next general elections, by offering positions to and ended the cooperative scheme. Later, lands became barren and 90 per cent of the Dalit families migrated to Chennai.

Ponugutivalasa is a village adjacent to Rajaam, a Mandal headquarter. This village was under the jurisdiction of Santhakaviti Mandal. In the post 90s, Rajaam became an industrial town under the aegis of the world famous GMR group. In Ponugutivalasa village, the government distributed the lands to Dalit families during the early 70s. It was also a rain-fed village and the land could not fetch livelihoods for them. To get rid of the debt burden, they sold the lands at throwaway prices. A son of a rich peasant became a doctor during the late 60s, and he emerged as a district officer in the health department. He bought most of the lands in the village. Now, because of the industries around, the land rates skyrocketed. To sum up, the rich peasant turned-bureaucrat reaped the maximum benefit from the land distribution.

Though it was peculiar to hear, in some villages, the government schemes had made the Dalits leave their lands. These examples present this peculiar outcome.

Sirusuvada is a village in Kothuru Mandal where the government allotted barren lands to 50 Dalit families, and they toiled hard to make them cultivable. Then the government took over some of this land to build houses for the backward classes. Some land was acquired to build a flood channel to Vamshadhara Phase II reservoir.

Annavaram is a village in Palakonda Mandal where the government allotted river Poramboku lands to the Dalit families who also brought waste lands into cultivation. They even installed bore wells for the fields, planted cashew and mango groves in those lands, and reaped the benefits. In the year 1990, floods of the river Nagavali inundated the lands The government is still building a retaining wall to Nagavali, which would flood almost every year. In this process, all the lands of Dalits are swamped by the river and became unworthy of cultivation.

Gochekka was a village in Parvathipuram Mandal. As mentioned earlier, the Mandal was 100 per cent rain-fed. Not only in Gochekka but in many villages of this Mandal too, the villagers had lost their lands to capitalist farmers. The capitalist farmers include the professionals of the peasant castes and settlers from other districts. It was one of the strange examples of the land alienation. The Dalits had sold the assigned lands to repay the debts that were caused by another government scheme. The government purchased the land from a Kamma settler through a Scheduled Caste corporation and distributed two acres each in which cashew plantations were raised. Dalits benefited from this land distribution. After the 2009 elections, the government sanctioned houses under the housing scheme to Dalits, called Indira Awas Yojana. The amount sanctioned under the scheme was insufficient to complete the construction and hence they took loans. By the time of completing the houses, the mounting debt burden made them sell the lands to another Kshatriya settled farmer.

Dalits and Attached Labour: Escape from Servitude

The prominent labour system that prevailed possibly over a century or more in Indian agriculture is the annual farm servant system or otherwise known as attached labour system. Here a labourer is given an annual wage as advance/credit, lead them into a debt trap by lending money at usurious interest rates, and thereby enjoy unfettered labour supply for ruthless exploitation. There was no alternative to selling for labour for rural Dalits who never owned and cultivated any land. Since the agrarian labour was seasonal in nature, Dalits had to opt for the attached labour system as an insurance mechanism under starvation, as it includes daily provision of food. An attached labourer in Srikakulam is called *Kambari*, and elsewhere he is referred to as *Paleru*. Besides Dalits, several other landless people of different castes also worked as attached labour in this district, while we can say Dalits constituted a dominant share of attached labour.

Rakesh Basant in his detailed study on the attached labour during the early 80s in India, observed: "In so far as the socially and economically handicapped Scheduled Castes, Scheduled Tribes and other backward castes acquiring the bulk of the attached labour contracts, and their employers are large farmers the latter may be in a position to pay them lower wage rates and/or depress the effective wage rates for this category of workers by extracting longer hours or more arduous work." Further, he noted it adversely affects the wages of the casual workers by reducing their bargaining power. In other words, for an employment security, labour foregoes value disproportionately ('Attached and Casual Labour Wage Rates' by Rakesh Basant, *Economic and Political Weekly*, March 3, 1984 p. 393). The employer gains unlimited capacity over fixing the labour power in the attached labour system.

During the early 70s, the kind wage paid was 180 kilograms of grain. The measurements were faulty. The employer though fed the attached labour three times a day, but always gave atrociously inferior quality food. Some rich peasants used to lure the labour with 10 cents of land to the attached labour and the yield on that to be given to him. It maintained the Dalit families barely above the starvation reserve, besides supplying the child labour for household chores of rich peasants. This child labour also were cattle grazers, only to graduate later into attached labour. The wives of the attached labour used to work in houses as house cleaners and in farmyards just to get some pickle for a meal at the end of the day. To put it briefly, the total family of the labourer is attached to the rich peasant manor, a stable job to insure against an otherwise full level starvation.

During 1960-67, the then Communist Party of India and Communist Party of India Marxist, CPI (M) tried to organize against the attached labour system in this district. But their influence was limited to a few places in the plains areas and slightly more in tribal tracts. After that for a very long period during 1968-82, there was hardly any agitation opposing attached labour. The economic and social oppression of them knew no limits in the countryside. This exploitation went unchallenged for about three decades.

When they were asked the reason for opting for such a hard and menial profession, a former attached labour aged about 80 years in Kanugula Valasa village replied: "Hunger! We were famished. Even we had dreams about taking food. When we were going along the riverside, there were sand dunes. We always used to dream if these sand dunes could transform as a heap of rice to enable us to eat voraciously."

The ushering of capitalist relations in the shape of transport, communication, education and electricity, etc. had paved the way for freeing these semi-serfs from the clutches of rich peasantry. The alternate employment opportunities that followed with the self-consciousness liberated them from the iron grip of rich peasants. The retreat slowly started during the late 80s in this district, and it reached its peak during the late 90s. By the turn of the 21st century, attached labour had almost disappeared from the countryside. In fact, it was a decisive victory of the new opportunities over the outdated relations.

However, this disappearance of semi-slave labour caused heartburn in the medium and rich peasantry. When asked about the reasons for disappearance of this system, an octogenarian peasant-caste women in Dalaipeta village replied outraged, "Finish! The good old days have gone. Nowadays, these Dalits are not even listening to us. Earlier we used to compel the Dalits from their huts by 4 am–in case they were absent, we used to tie them to pillars and whip them". This statement represented the opinion of rural affluent sections.

In the villages surveyed, only in one village, an organization tried to organize the attached labour. Duggeru is a tribal hamlet in Makkuva Mandal. In this village, the association of peasants, labourers and poor people (Telugu Rythu Coolie Pedala Sangam, Andhra Pradesh) organized Adivasis and Dalits for seeking a hike in the wages of attached labour and achieved a partial success. However, by that time, the profession as a whole waned out in the remaining broad plain areas.

Rural Wage Rates

For a very long time, the village rich peasantry as monopoly buyers of agricultural labour decided the wages rates in the labour markets. Usurious interest rates were used to tie the agricultural labour to farms. Endless expropriation of surplus value is derived from this hapless class of agricultural labour. Even though Minimum Wage Acts were promulgated, neither did any labour unions work assiduously nor were the Dalit labour in a condition to understand and exercise their rights. The rich peasantry thus generated vast amounts of agrarian surplus and transferred them to build urban property and urban business. This has made the cheap raw material for agro-industry and cheapened the wages in industry. There is a continuum in surplus value produced in rural areas, transferred to urban area and reproduced at an expanded level. Ironically, the opportunities created in the urban expanded reproduction of surplus labour, in turn began creating opportunities for Dalit labour to escape the village oppression.

For a very long time rural real wage rates stagnated. Including the villages surveyed, one does not hear that any united struggles for the wages of the rural proletariat that took place in this district. The late professor G. Parthasarathy made an astute observation:

"Despite the considerable rise in money wages, real wages of agriculture labour in Andhra Pradesh are marked by stagnation. There is no association between trends in real wages and per capita (rural) agricultural production. The picture of stagnation at the state level applies also to mostly all districts. A noteworthy aspect of the data is the negative, though not statistically significant, trend in real wages for a relatively well developed district such as West Godavari which is known to have experienced significant changes in technology" (Real Wages of Agricultural Labour in Andhra Pradesh: Two Decades of Stagnation by G. Parthasarathy, *Economic and Political Weekly*, July 31, 1982, p. 1248). There were no unions for them. The rural labour enquiry of 1974-75 remark that, "only 1 per cent of agricultural labourers were members of any organization or union of farm labourers" (*EPW*, June 14-21, 1980, p. 1045) becomes applicable for this district too. Increase in productivity does not automatically increase real wages.

The small peasantry rallying behind the rich peasantry unfortunately emboldens the latter in curbing the voice of the rural proletarian. Not only are peasants divided on caste lines, agrarian labour too are divided on the same lines. In some villages they have their caste associations. However, when it comes to work, they all demand the same level of wages.

The decade of 2000s saw some faster growth of nominal wages, particularly after 2007. Many scholars attributed this to the implementation of the Mahatma Gandhi National Rural Employment Act. But in Srikakulam district, rural wages began rising even before. Though the rich peasantry complain about the exorbitant growth in the wage rates, the actual growth in the real terms is still nominal. The main reason for the stagnation lay in the disunity among the vastly scattered masses. The labour is getting feminized every day. In Srikakulam district, it is only men who migrate mostly, even among the Dalits. It is the female labour that still bears the yoke of agricultural labour in the countryside. Female wages are far less than male wages. The out migration of male labour has forced the rich peasantry to quickly resort to mechanization. The withdrawal of agrarian labour because of migration led to the wage rise in the countryside which remained above starvation reserve for such a long time.

From Agricultural Labour to Urban Migrant Labour

Dalits in the village by default became agricultural labour, not cultivators. They were attached labour at some point. But they could come out of its clutches and become casual labour. Yet the majority were still situated in agriculture. While the backward caste labour migrated as agricultural labour to wetland labour during the Green Revolution phase in south coastal Andhra districts, Dalits still could not migrate much. This began changing by the early 1990s. The opportunity that the construction sector in the country offered a major opportunity for the Dalits in this region to escape the tyranny of the village and earn a far better wage income.

The percentage of Dalit agrarian proletariat among Dalit main workers in the district recorded as 69.76 in 1961, increased to 75 per cent in 1991, but by 2001 it dropped to 69.70 per cent. The agrarian labour in general drastically decreased during 1991-2001 to 27.35. It is interesting to observe that even the main workers in agriculture in general began showing a decreasing trend. Dalits who had to earn their livelihood as workers, began leaving the villages, to avoid the obnoxious circumstances conditioned by laws of Manu. Those Dalits who chose to become farmers face the damning prospects offered by market forces.

REFERENCES

Ambedkar, B.R., 2010. *Essays on Untouchables and Untouchability: Social.* www.ambedkar.org.

Vidyasagar, S.R., 2014. *Voices Unheard*, Gyan Publishers, New Delhi.

Parthasarathy, B., 2002. "Changing Agrarian Structure and Nature of Transition in the Post-Green Revolution Period" in Krishna Rao, Y.V. and Subrahmanyam edited *Development of Andhra Pradesh: 1956-2001: A Study of Regional Disparities*, NRR Research Centre, Hyderabad.

Basant, Rakesh, 1984. 'Attached and Casual Labour Wage Rates', *Economic and Political Weekly*, Vol. 19, Issue No. 9, March.

16

The Nationalization of the Land

[Karl Marx[1]]

The property in the soil is the original source of all wealth, and has become the great problem upon the solution of which depends the future of the working class.

I do not intend discussing here all the arguments put forward by the advocates of private property in land, by jurists, philosophers and political economists, but shall confine myself firstly to state that they have tried hard to disguise the primitive fact of conquest under the cloak of *"Natural Right"*. If conquest constituted a natural right on the part of the few, the many have only to gather sufficient strength in order to acquire the natural right of reconquering what has been taken from them.

In the progress of history the conquerors found it convenient to give to their original titles, derived from brute force, a sort of social standing through the instrumentality of laws imposed by themselves.

At last comes the philosopher and demonstrates that those laws imply and express the universal consent of mankind. If private property in land is indeed founded upon such an universal consent, it will evidently become extinct from the moment the majority of a society dissent from warranting it.

However, leaving aside the so-called "rights" of property, I assert that the economic development of society, the increase and concentration of people, the very circumstances that compel the capitalist farmer to apply to an agriculture collective and organized labour, and to have recourse to machinery and similar contrivances, will increasingly render the nationalization of land a "Social Necessity", against which no amount of talk about the rights of property can be of any avail. The imperative wants of society will and must be satisfied, changes dictated by social necessity will work their own way, and sooner or later adapt legislation to their interests.

What we require is a daily increasing production and its exigencies cannot be met by allowing a few individuals to regulate it according to their whims and private interests, or to ignorantly exhaust the powers of the soil. All modern methods, such as irrigation, drainage, steam ploughing, chemical treatment and so forth, ought to be applied to agriculture at large. But the scientific knowledge we possess, and the technical means of agriculture we command, such as machinery, etc., can never be successfully applied but by cultivating the land on a large scale.

If cultivation on a large scale proves (even under its present capitalist form, that degrades the cultivator himself to a mere beast of burden) so superior, from an economic point of view, to small and piecemeal husbandry, would it not give an increased impulse to production if applied on national dimensions?

The ever-growing wants of the people on the one side, the ever-increasing price of agricultural produce on the other, afford the irrefutable evidence that the nationalization of land has become a social necessity.

Such a diminution of agricultural produce as springs from individual abuse, will, of course, become impossible whenever cultivation is carried on under the control and for the benefit of the nation.

All the citizens I have heard here today during the progress of the debate, on this question, defended the nationalization of land, but they took very different views of it.

France was frequently alluded to, but with its *peasant proprietorship* it is farther off the nationalization of land than

England with its landlordism. In France, it is true, the soil is accessible to all who can buy it, but this very facility has brought about a division into small plots cultivated by men with small means and mainly relying upon the land by exertions of themselves and their families. This form of landed property and the piecemeal cultivation it necessitates, while excluding all appliances of modern agricultural improvements, converts the tiller himself into the most decided enemy to social progress and, above all, the nationalization of land. Enchained to the soil upon which he has to spend all his vital energies in order to get a relatively small return, having to give away the greater part of his produce to the state, in the form of taxes, to the law tribe in the form of judiciary costs, and to the usurer in the form of interest, utterly ignorant of the social movements outside his petty field of employment; still he clings with fanatic fondness to his bit of land and his merely nominal proprietorship in the same. In this way the French peasant has been thrown into a most fatal antagonism to the industrial working class.

Peasant proprietorship being then the greatest obstacle to the nationalization of land, France, in its present state, is certainly not the place where we must look to for a solution of this great problem.

To nationalize the land, in order to let it out in small plots to individuals or working men's societies, would, under a middle-class government, only engender a reckless competition among themselves and thus result in a progressive increase of "Rent" which, in its turn, would afford new facilities to the appropriators of feeding upon the producers.

At the International Congress of Brussels, in 1868, one of our friends [César De Paepe, in his report on land property: meeting of the Brussels Congress of the International Working Men's Association of September 11, 1868] said:

> Small private property in land is doomed by the verdict of science, large land property by that of justice. There remains then only one alternative. The soil must become the property of rural associations or the property of the whole nation. The future will decide that question.

I say on the contrary; the social movement will lead to this decision that the land can only be owned by the nation itself. To give up the soil to the hands of associated rural labourers, would be to surrender society to one exclusive class of producers.

The nationalization of land will work a complete change in the relations between labour and capital, and finally, do away with the capitalist form of production, whether industrial or rural. Then class distinctions and privileges will disappear together with the economic basis upon which they rest. To live on other people's labour will become a thing of the past. There will no longer be any government or state power, distinct from society itself. Agriculture, mining, manufacture, in one word, all branches of production, will gradually be organized in the most adequate manner. National centralization of the means of production will become the national basis of a society composed of associations of free and equal producers, carrying on the social business on a common and rational plan. Such is the humanitarian goal to which the great economic movement of the 19th century is tending.

About the Contributors

Amit Basole is an Associate Professor at the School of Liberal Studies, Azim Premji University, Bangalore, India.

Cristobal Kay is an Emeritus Professor at the International Institute of Social Studies (ISS), The Hague, Erasmus University Rotterdam, Netherland.

Deepankar Basu is an Associate Professor at the Department of Economics, University of Massachusetts, Amherst, USA.

Friedrich Engels (1820-1895) was a German philosopher, communist and political companion of Karl Marx.

Haroon Akram-Lodhi is a Professor of International Development Studies at Trent University, Peterborough, Canada.

Henry Bernstein is an Emeritus Professor of Development Studies at the School of Oriental and African Studies, University of London.

Jens Lerche is a Reader in School of Oriental and African Studies, University of London, UK.

Kalyan Sanyal (1955-2012) was a Professor of Economics, University of Calcutta, India.

Karl Kautsky (1854-1938) was a Marxist scholar and theoretician for Social Democratic Party, Germany.

Karl Marx (1818-1883) was a German philosopher, political economist, and socialist revolutionary.

Praful Bidwai (1949-2015) was an Indian journalist and left political analyst.

R.V. Ramana Murthy is a Professor at the School of Economics, University of Hyderabad, India.

S.R. Vidyasagar is a Marxist scholar at the Centre for Independent Research (CFIR), Vishakhapatnam, India.

Stephan R. Epstein (1960-2007) was a Professor of History, London School of Economics, UK.

Terence J. Byres is an Emeritus Professor at the School of Oriental and African Studies, University of London.